IRISH JOURNEY

IRISH JOURNEY

BY

HALLIDAY SUTHERLAND

THE DEVIN-ADAIR COMPANY
NEW YORK, 1958

TO THE MEMORY OF
DENIS VALENTINE MORRIS
PROFESSOR OF OBSTETRICS AND GYNAECOLOGY
IN THE UNIVERSITY OF GALWAY

Born—14th February, 1889
Died—3rd July, 1941
Requiescat in Pace

Preface to the American Edition

I declined to write about Ireland when, in 1937, I was invited to do so by my friend the late Professor Morris of Galway University. I told him that no one could write a book about Ireland without getting into trouble. How right I was. In 1955 I wrote *Irish Journey* and this book has been damned by faint praise from every newspaper critic in Ireland. I was not surprised, because all the critics have ignored my main criticism, which concerns the Irish secular clergy. In my opinion they have too much political power. They hold themselves aloof from their people, and are too fond of money.

In the bad old days, when Ireland was subject to the foreign power of England, the parish priest was probably the only educated man in an Irish village. The foreign power has been driven out, the people are better educated, but the parish priest is loathe to relinquish his political power.

During my Irish holiday, I was assaulted by a total stranger in a Tipperary hotel. The incident was reported in all the Dublin papers, and when I returned to my Dublin hotel, the receptionist said to me, "Will you be writing about it?" I told her I would, and she replied, "That won't be nice." She was obviously afraid that the record of this incident would spoil Ireland as a show place.

Ireland is certainly a wonderful show place, and heaven may reflect Killarney; but as a Scotsman I think Loch Lomond, twenty miles from Glasgow, is more beautiful.

Another day, a well-known man called at the hotel to see me. I met him in the lounge, but he asked me out to his car. I asked him where were we going and he said, "Nowhere, but there were too many people in the lounge who might overhear what I am going to ask you, and that is not to mention me in your book."

"And why not?"

"They wouldn't like it."

I know that he meant the Irish hierarchy. It is strange how the shadow of the hierarchy falls on the most unexpected places in the public life of Ireland.

If Ireland goes communist within the next ten years, I think the secular clergy will be to blame.

The *Catholic Medical Guardian* of London gave my book an excellent review and said that my account of the assault on myself in a Tipperary hotel recalled the best chapters in *Handy Andy*. But a copy of my book was sent to a nun in Dublin who replied, "This book should be burnt by the public hangman."

I only hope that what I have written will be more appreciated in the clearer air of the United States of America.

HALLIDAY SUTHERLAND

Kensington
July, 1958

CONTENTS

N

Donegal

Belfast

Sligo

Donamon

Roscommon

Tuam

Dublin

L. CORRIB

Clifden

Galway

Loughrea

Birr

Portumna

Roscrea

Limerick

Tralee

Doneraile

Mt. Melleray

Killarney

Mallow

GAP OF
DUNLOE

Muckross Abbey

Cork

Cobh

Kinsale

Miles

0   20   40   60   80

——————— RAIL JOURNEYS   ·········· MOTOR JOURNEYS

CHAPTER I

The Invitation

"WHY don't you write a book about Ireland?"

My questioner was Professor Morris who had the Chair of Obstetrics and Gynaecology in the University of Galway. He was a broad-shouldered middle-aged man of medium height, clean-shaven with iron grey hair. He was a widower with four young children. The year was 1937. He had come to England on business that took him to the Doncaster Races, and on the return journey he called at my house in Kensington to ask the question to which I replied: "No one can write about Ireland without getting into trouble."

"Come to Galway as my guest. You can stay at Glen Nina—that's my house—for as long as you like. Make it your headquarters. Write the book and let them say what they like."

I thanked him and said I would think it over. This was our first and last meeting.

In August of that year my daughter and her brother Peter, both in their teens, were on a walking tour in Ireland. In the city of Galway they found simple lodgings and then called at the Professor's consulting-rooms where they left their address and my letter of introduction. Next morning the Professor came to their lodging and motored them and their rucksacks to Glen Nina some three miles on the Dublin road beyond the city. There they stayed for three happy weeks. It was a large two-storied house standing in four acres of ground. From the lodge gates on the Dublin road a drive crossed a large paddock to another gate that gave entrance to the grounds around the house. The lodge-keeper and his wife lived rent free. Their duty was to open the gate for the Professor's car up to 11 p.m. After that time when called to his nursing home in Galway, he himself opened the gate. During the day the paddock was usually occupied by the Professor's race-horse. In no circumstances was that animal to be disturbed. If it was grazing at one end of the paddock the Professor's children— a boy and three girls—had to play at the other end. A groom looked after the race-horse and the garden. The indoor staff were a cook-housekeeper and a general servant. One morning at breakfast they gave notice. The Professor was very annoyed—"I pay you good wages. I give you everything you ask for housekeeping. Yet you must quarrel and give me notice. It's too bad." By 4 p.m. the quarrel was made up and their notices withdrawn.

At 10.30 a.m. on a bright and sunny morning my daughter from a rowing-boat on Loch Corrib in the presence of the Professor, his son Jim, and Peter, caught her first trout. It weighed half a pound. The Professor said: "If my wife were alive we would now row to the shore, light a fire, and clean and cook the trout." Often that morning he gazed at the surrounding mountains. He was looking for that wisp of smoke that would betray the site of a poteen or illicit still. That morning the still was not working, but some years earlier all Galway had laughed on hearing that their Chief of Police had unwittingly safely delivered to one of the Professor's friends in Dublin a bottle of poteen to which a medicine label had been attached.

One night in August 1938 I was writing in my library when the telephone rang. It was Professor Morris. He was telephoning from Galway. "How are things in London?"

"Not too good. There are trenches in Hyde Park and they've brought an anti-aircraft gun from the Victoria and Albert Museum. Some bits are supposed to be missing so that it can't be fired."

"Look here. Why don't you bring your wife and family to Glen Nina. There's plenty of room and lots of food. You could write a book about Ireland. Can you hear me, doctor?"

I had heard, but for the moment was overwhelmed by his kindness. Then I answered: "Thank you. In the event of war I accept for my wife and family. For myself I'll try to rejoin the Navy. If anything happens I hope you'll look after them."

"If anything happens to you I'll look after them as though they were my own."

"Thank you very much."

That was my last conversation with the most generous Irishman I had ever known.

Then came Mr. Chamberlain's visit to Hitler at Munich and I forgot all about the Professor until the end of August 1939. I was on my way to Australia where I wrote *Southward Journey*.

I had sailed from Tilbury in the s.s. *Maloja*. One morning in the Mediterranean I took an early walk on deck and passed an elderly Brahmin to whom I said "Good morning". He made no reply, but raised his right hand in which he carried a string of beads. Later in the day he apologised for not having answered, and explained the reason, lest I should think him discourteous. I in turn apologised for not having recognised that he was saying his prayers. Thus I became friendly with a very able man who held high office in India. He was a member of the Viceroy's Council. One conversation in particular I do remember.

"In relation to religions," he said, "what people do you think are the most truthful?"

"I've no idea."

"Well, in my experience Mohammedans are the most truthful. They really live by the Koran and know it by heart. Next in truthfulness I would put the Christians."

"Not the Hindus?"

"No"—and he slowly shook his head. "There is too much formalism in our religion. For example on this ship, it is quite impossible for me to practise all the details of my religion. Yet at daybreak, noon, afternoon and nightfall, you will see these Lascars with their praying mats on the fo'c'sle. As a Catholic you can hear Mass if there be a priest on board; and if not you can say your prayers and abstain from meat on Fridays. With us Hindus it is different."

One evening in reply to my question about the likelihood of war, he said: "Tomorrow morning at 5 a.m. we shall be at Port Said for three or four hours. Some representatives from the oil companies are coming on board to see me. If you're on deck at six o'clock you can hear what they've got to say."

At 6 a.m. I found him talking to three Englishmen, to whom I was introduced. One of them told me that six British destroyers had just gone through the Suez Canal ahead of the *Maloja*. He then led me to the ship's rail. "You see that boy selling oranges on the quay. If you buy one of his oranges you must eat it on the spot. You are not allowed to bring it on board."

"And why not?"

"Because at midnight an order was signed prohibiting the export of all food from Egypt."

I thanked him for the information and went ashore to the Post Office from which I sent the following cable to my wife—"All of you are to leave at once for Galway." The day was Wednesday, 30th August, 1939.

Before sending that cablegram I had remembered that someone in authority—I think it was the Commissioner of Police—had prophesied that an air raid on London would leave thirty thousand dead. To my mind this meant that the dead would be cremated in our public parks. Little did I know that there would be no air raids on London until I returned in nine months' time. Then as an air-raid warden I was to see more war in Kensington W. 8. than I had ever seen in the Navy. On this occasion the Admiralty had decided that I was too old for the Navy.

My cablegram was delivered, but it was my daughter who led the opposition to my wishes: "No, I am not going to Ireland until the Irish stop leaving explosives in suit-cases at English railway stations."

It is seventeen years since Professor Morris invited me to write this book, and now at long last the writing has begun.

CHAPTER II

At the Coombe Lying-in Hospital

In 1904 I was a fourth year medical student at Edinburgh University, and in August of that year I went to Dublin for a month's practical midwifery at the Coombe Hospital. I was then aged 22, and travelled third class via Stranraer and Belfast. The steamer arrived at Belfast on the morning of Sunday, August 9th, and I carried my luggage to the railway station. There I was told by a porter that there were no Sunday trains to Dublin. Yet, at one platform stood a train whose carriage windows bore the placards—*The Happy Life*. I asked the porter what it was and where it was going.

"Theatre special for Dublin. Maybe they'd let you travel."

At the luggage van, I found a large fat man who wore a broad-rimmed hat and an overcoat with an astrakhan collar. He was supervising the loading of scenery and I asked him if I might travel to Dublin?

"Got a ticket, laddie? Third class, well there's plenty of room. You can find a seat."

I walked forward and passed a first-class carriage at the door of which stood a beautiful blonde in a fur coat. She must have been the leading lady. Finally I found a third-class carriage with two junior actors. They were quite pleasant but had little to say and played cards with each other almost all the way to Dublin, a three hours' journey. At Amiens Street Station, Dublin, I thanked the stage manager for allowing me to travel by special train—"You're welcome, laddie. Come and see the show. Ask for me and I will pass you in."

Alas, I never saw *The Happy Life*. There was too much to do at the Coombe.

From Amiens Street Station I drove to the Hospital, a distance of one mile in a jaunting-car, also called a side-car. This was a one-horsed, two-wheeled vehicle. The jarvey or driver sat in the front. Behind him two seats ran backwards the length of the car. Two passengers could sit on each seat with their feet on a step that overhung the side of the car and the top of the wheel. The two passengers on one side were back to back against the two on the other side. Today, the only jaunting-cars in Eire are to be seen on the roads around the lakes of Killarney. The jarveys apparently think it is the duty of the Government to preserve them and their jaunting-cars like ancient monuments.

The Hospital is in the Coombe, on the main street of the Coombe district which forms part of the south quarter of the city near the great Guinness Brewery. Beside the main gate is the hospital to the right of which three buildings overlook an asphalted courtyard. Of these the first is the White House, the second is the Gynaecological Department, and the third is the Students' Common Room.

The assistant porter, whose name was Glasgow, carried my bag upstairs to the first floor of the White House where two large rooms were subdivided into cubicles, fifteen in all. Each contained a bed, a small chest of drawers, a looking-glass, and an iron stand with basin, jug, soap and towel. I do not know why this building was called "The White House." It may have been white when built in 1826. It was not white in 1904, and was less white when I saw it in 1955. A benefactor named White may have endowed it! In the White House were two old-fashioned baths with mid-Victorian fittings. There were ten more cubicles in another building called the Canteen. I had sent my entrance fee of 10s. 6d. on the 10th April, and now paid four guineas to the Registrar for four weeks' tuition. Food was an extra, but

7

one's mess bills were usually less than a pound a week. Tuition fees are now eight guineas.

In the Hospital in 1904, there was one large ward of 45 beds. When the pains of labour began, the woman was moved to a smaller waiting ward of six beds. Here she remained until "the waters had broken." Before birth every child is surrounded by a fluid contained in a sac called the amnion. Under pressure from the labour pains, caused by contractions of the womb, the sac ruptures, usually in front of the child's head. The woman was then moved into the Labour ward in which there were two beds, or couches on which the babies were born.

In some cases the sac may rupture over another part of the child's body. Then the child may be born with the amnion round its head. In popular language such a child is born with a caul. Amongst sailors there is widespread belief that to possess a caul is a protection against death by drowning. I fear the unscrupulous medical students have sold to simple sailors many amnions that were never cauls.

I spent most of my first week in the Labour ward. Here I saw the final act in Nature's most stupendous mystery— The reproduction of species. Here I saw how babies are born. The foal, a few minutes after birth, is on its feet and ready as in ancient days to follow the herd if pursued by wolves; but the child, the only animal with a soul, or if you boggle over that, then the only animal with the gift of creative intelligence, is at birth the most helpless of living things. Then one of the sisters showed me how to assist a woman during confinement. When a child is born it is attached to the mother by the umbilical cord and usually gives a cry. In that event you leave the child so attached until the vessel in the cord has ceased to beat. You then tie and cut the cord. This means that the child starts life with a full supply of blood.

When the child is born, you place your hand on the woman's abdomen. Beneath your palm, you can feel the upper border of the womb upon which you may keep your hand until the afterbirth is separated. This usually occurs from ten to thirty minutes after the birth of the child. When the placenta separates, you effect its expulsion by pressing the womb downwards and backwards. That is the Dublin method. When the afterbirth is expelled, you give the woman a dose of ergot. This causes the womb to contract and helps to prevent haemorrhage. Then you are happy. Ergot is obtained from the black parasite of that name which grows on barley. It is cultivated in Georgia in U.S.S.R. During World War II it was in short supply and a dose cost as much as ten shillings. Ergot is now given by injection intramuscularly or intravenously.

The purpose of keeping your hand on the abdomen is not to assist the separation of the afterbirth, but to enable you to detect any sudden dilatation of the womb. This would be the first sign of post-partum haemorrhage from which, unless you act quickly, a woman may bleed to death within a few minutes. I have never seen this dread sequel of childbirth. Fortunately, it is rare nowadays. Among 3,749 women delivered within the Coombe Hospital or on its district in 1953, there was no death from post-partum haemorrhage. The pub past the hospital is known to all the Coombe students as the P.P.H. The local inhabitants also know it by this title although I do not suppose they know the dire significance of these initials.

The Coombe Hospital is now very overcrowded. This is not surprising. At the beginning of the century, the population of Dublin was 200,000. By 1955 it had increased to 550,000. Thanks to the Irish Hospitals' Sweep, a new Coombe Lying-in Hospital will soon be built in an adjacent street, at a cost of one million sterling. Despite the overcrowding, the neo-natal mortality at the Coombe is the lowest in Dublin. Of babies born alive in the service of the hospital in 1953, only 2·4 per cent died within thirty days of birth. This low mortality I attribute in part to the old-fashioned custom of placing the newly-born babies in bed with their mothers. This was what Nature intended. In my recent visit, however, I asked some of the mothers where the baby would sleep when they went home. Some of them replied: "In a cot at the foot of my bed." Breast-feeding is dying out.

Dr. Kevin Feeney, the present Master of the Coombe, showed me round the hospital. He told me of one change in practice. The new-born baby is no longer washed. The vernix or natural grease is left on its skin. This keeps the baby warm and protects the skin against infection. As we looked at the old-fashioned cubicles he said: "Many of the men who slept there have become great obstetricians or gynaecologists." That was true because the Coombe has always had a world-wide reputation as a great teaching hospital. I asked him if there was much difference between the students of today and those of fifty years ago. He replied: "I think they work harder and drink less than you did, but I don't think they have such a good time. The curriculum is so full that they have more lectures and more reading. Drink is so expensive that they cannot afford it."

I was alone when I attended my first case on the district. It was in a room on the first floor of a large tenement. The woman fully dressed lay on straw in a corner. The only furniture was a chair on which was placed an empty basin. The husband, a little man, was drunk. I asked him to fetch a kettle of boiling water. Leaving the door open he made his way down the stone stairs. Half-way down he met his mother-in-law carrying a kettle. He tried to take the kettle from her. She refused. They struggled and both fell down the stairs. When they got up they fought like cat and dog. There were curses and screams. The uproar brought the police. Finally a policeman entered the room. I told him the woman in the corner was going to have a baby and asked him to fetch a kettle of boiling water. This he did. When he came back, he informed me that the husband had been arrested for being drunk and disorderly, and the mother-in-law had been taken to hospital to have stitches inserted in her head. He remained and assisted me with the confinement. When that was over, the baby, the policeman, and myself were the only sober persons in the room. Even the poor mother was slightly inebriated. Sean O'Casey has not exaggerated the poverty and drunkenness in Dublin slums at the beginning of the century.

I was also alone at my second case. Here the child was born with asphyxia. It was not breathing and the skin was blue. This called for artificial respiration. I held the baby in front of me, with its back towards me, and its arms by its side. I grasped it by the upper arms with my fingers on its back. By suddenly bending my arms, the baby was jerked upwards and backwards so that the feet were thrown over the head. When I stretched my arms the baby was also extended. After half a dozen such movements the child began to breathe and the pink colour returned to its skin. The patient's mother had left the room when I began artificial respiration. She now returned with a bowl of water and asked me to baptise the child. I told her the baby was all right and could be baptised later, but she begged me to do it. So I sprinkled some of the water on the child's head as I had seen ministers do in Scotland. This did not satisfy the grandmother who tipped the bowl so that the water—it may have been Holy Water—poured over the child's head. Then I said: "I baptise you Patrick Dooey in the Name of the Father and of the Son and of the Holy Ghost."

At the time I wondered if the baptism was valid. I had been brought up a Scots Presbyterian, but now was in theory an agnostic and in practice an atheist. Sixteen years later, Fr. Joseph Keating, S. J. received me into the Catholic Church at Farm Street, London. Then I learnt that in case of emergency anyone, even an atheist, may baptise a child provided he has the intention of doing so. The saying of the words shows his intention, even if he does not believe in baptism.

After that, I worked with a lady medical student from Glasgow. She was a tall girl. It was her intention to become a medical missionary. One Saturday afternoon I took her to see the British Fleet in Dublin Bay. On that occasion I thought she was too archly coy.

One day we were at a case where I thought the midwifery forceps should be used. I sent to the hospital for one of the resident tutors. We were not allowed to use forceps except by permission and in the presence of a qualified doctor. He came and agreed. The patient lay across the bed and I administered chloroform. It was the lady student's turn to apply the forceps. She sterilised them in a small steriliser heated by methylated spirit. As she was carrying the forceps towards the bed, she suddenly dropped them on the floor, threw herself on the patient, kissed her and cried, "Poor Anna, poor Anna." I did not know the patient's name was Anna. The tutor swore and ordered her to leave the house. He then gave the anaesthetic. I reboiled the instruments and delivered the patient.

One morning we made a routine visit to a house in which three days earlier we had delivered one of our patients. The grandmother opened the door and said, "Good mornin', miss, I see you're still with Dr. Sutherland." "I assure you I hardly know Dr. Sutherland." "Sure, miss, and they say ye never knows a man until ye get into bed with him."

These old women of Dublin were very homely. They did not like lady doctors. They used to call me 'Dr. Jewel' and I thought they did not know my name. Then I learnt that 'Jewel' was the anglicised form of an Irish term of endearment. They said 'Doctor Jewel' as they might have said 'Doctor dear'. Sometimes they spoke of the time when there had been "A little bit of truble at the Coombe". I found that this referred to 1893 when the Master of the Coombe was in love with the matron on whom he performed an illegal operation from which she died. He was not tried, but he had to resign the Mastership of the Coombe.

On our last night at the Coombe we had a smoking concert. This was attended by the Master, Dr. Stevens, and by Dr. Michael Gibson, the Assistant Master. The lady medicals were not invited. We drank beer and to the tune of "There is a Tavern in the Town" we sang that rousing song of which I now remember only the chorus:

> Bear down, bear down, good Mrs. Brown
> Bear down, bear down
> I've got my finger on his crown
> On his crown
> And soon I'll pull the little beggar down
> Bear down, good Mrs. Brown
> Bear down, bear down.

At midnight our guests had difficulty in departing. Many of the students lay down in front of the motor-cars. Those of us who were less drunk had to persuade them to rise and let the cars proceed. On returning to Edinburgh I started a Coombe Dinner. This was attended by the Master, and the Assistant Master. They met their old pupils and also prospective pupils. The dinner no longer survives.

With two other Edinburgh medical students I made several excursions from the Coombe. On a Saturday afternoon we went to Leopardstown Race-course, six miles from the centre of Dublin. We drove there in a jaunting-car. We had one of the morning papers which told us which horses to back. It was an off day for the racing prophet of that paper. In the silver ring we landed five consecutive losers. For the last race we pooled our money, mostly in sixpences and pennies. If the horse won we would win not a fortune, but the price of a jaunting-car home. The animal lost, and so we walked six miles to Dublin and then a further mile to the Coombe.

Next day I told Dr. Michael Gibson, the Assistant Master, of our unfortunate outing. "Why did you not tell me you were going? There was room for all of you in my car, I was there and won thirty pounds." He was a kind man. He was Master from 1907 to 1914. Then he came to England where he died in 1951. In Dublin he is remembered as one of the greatest Masters of the Coombe.

Why had we not told him we were going to Leopardstown? Because we were three Scots, and had been brought up in the tradition that betting, drink and fornication were all equally reprehensible. Little did we know Ireland. A love of horses and of betting is inborn in every Irishman. Fifty per cent of them are total abstainers and fornication is a mortal sin.

Irish priests are forbidden by their bishops to attend race meetings in Ireland. This is reputed to be due to the mistake of one Dublin priest in the pulpit. He had given a trusted parishioner a large sum of money to be put on a horse at Leopardstown. The horse won, but the parishioner did not return. One day the priest was in the pulpit. What he intended saying was, "This is the fifth Sunday after Pentecost." What he did say in a sad voice was, "This is the fifth Sunday after Leopards . . ." Priests are now forbidden to attend race meetings in Ireland, but every year they come to Aintree in their hundreds. Were I an artist I would draw a picture of what happened at one Grand National when a horse threw its rider at the first fence and the entire grand stand rose to pronounce conditional absolution.

Thirty-one years later I was once more at Leopardstown and learnt the only possible way of winning money on this or any other race-course.

One evening we go to the Abbey Theatre. What the play is about I do not remember, this is not surprising. When the curtain falls on the first act, a general discussion begins in the audience. The discussion becomes acrimonious. All over the theatre men are standing. Blows are given and, I regret to say, received. We are in the centre block of the stalls. I am one seat from the gangway on the left. Next me on my left is a huge Irishman who looks like a heavy-weight boxer. He says the play is rotten. I say the first act is very good. Soon we are standing face to face. I tell him I am dramatic critic on the *Student*, the undergraduate magazine of Edinburgh University. This news annoys the man. He shouts, "To hell with you." He pulls me into the gangway. With his great fist he grabs the back of my coat collar. He propels me towards the exit, through the foyer and out of the theatre. At the top of the steps he gives me a dunt on the backside with his right knee. This sends me from the top of the steps to the pavement where I land on my back. From Rugby football I fortunately knew how to fall without breaking my bones. A tall Dublin Metropolitan policeman helps me to my feet. "Are ye hurt, sorr?"

"No, I am not hurt."

"Then stand out of the way. Here's another one coming."

I stand on the pavement until some fifty people including my two friends are ejected. We three, somewhat breathless and dishevelled, proceed to the nearest pub. We have all lost our hats in the mêlée. In the pub we drink Guinness. I say we have discovered Ireland. Those who liked the play were thrown out, those who disliked it stayed in the theatre. This must be typically Irish.

Having refreshed ourselves we walked along the street and were soon in conversation with a total stranger. He was a very decent Irishman who was horrified to hear of our adventure and invited us to his club. It was not in Kildare Street, but was quite a respectable place on the first floor of a building. Where the building was I do not know. I sat in the smoking-room where I had amicable conversation with a member who supplied me with refreshment. My two friends went with their host to the billiard-room, to have, as they said, a game of pills. Time passed pleasantly. Our host reappeared. He was leading one of my friends by the arm. The friend was smiling aimlessly. He was obviously well content. The host said, "I think you ought to go."

"Why should we go?"

"It's late and I think you've had enough."

"It's early, not late. We have not had enough. We never have enough. But I know when the laws of hospitality have been fractured. I came here with two friends. I do not leave without them. I see one of them. Where is the other?"

"He may have gone home."

"He may be murdered in the club."

"Now that's a bad thing to say."

"Then, let us search for the missing man."

This was echoed by four others in the smoking-room. We searched all over the club. One member in a lavatory was annoyed by the knocking on the door. He was indignant when asked for his name. Finally we entered the billiard-room. It was crowded, but none of them had seen our friend until I saw him under a billiard table. Willing hands pulled him out. More willing hands carried him downstairs into the street. There we got a jaunting-car. Two of us boarded it one on each side. Six members of the club heaved the limp body of our friend. We laid him face downwards across the car. I had the legs. My friend held the shoulders. We said good-bye to the members of the club who returned to their work. The jarvey turned round. "Is he dead, sorr?"

"Yes, dead drunk."

"Glory be. Where would ye be going?"

"The Coombe."

"The Coombe it is." And he whipped up his horse and rattled us over the now empty streets of sleeping Dublin. At the Coombe we unloaded our friend. With some difficulty we got him up the stairs of the White House and into his cubicle. Then we submitted him to the "last indignity". We put him to bed.

Recently I heard of a young man who went to confession to a dear old Irish priest in Birmingham. The young man accused himself of drunkenness.

"Did ye put yourself to bed?"

"Yes, Father."

"Then you weren't drunk."

If that were always true, I tremble to think of the false confessions I have made. But it is not always true and the old priest was being over-generous. Of course the man who puts his walking-stick to bed, and stands all night in the umbrella-stand is drunk, very drunk. But putting yourself to bed may be an automatic action which, like a conditioned reflex, is performed without the use of reason. Theologically you are only drunk when you have lost the use of reason. And how do you know when that happens? I once put that question to a priest in the Highlands of Scotland, and he replied, "You ken fine the next morn."

It is no use talking about being under the influence of drink. After one single glass everyone is under the influence. Usually this promotes a feeling of well-being, which the Greeks call Euphoria, and this promotes social intercourse. If anyone doubts this let him make an after-dinner speech at a banquet of total abstainers. I once did so. The result was disastrous. It caused a Jew to make a blasphemous speech in a Christian land. Most of the medical tests, including the blood test for drunkenness are also inadequate. It is no use asking a man to walk along a chalk line. Many people cannot do this when stone cold sober. Nor is it fair to ask him to repeat a tongue twister such as "The Leith Police dismisseth us", and the best test, provided there be no clock in the room, is to ask him to tell you the time without looking at his watch. If it be after midnight and he says it is 10 p.m. then he is drunk. Come to think of it I believe that a policeman is as good as any expert in deciding who is drunk.

One night we walked down Tyrone Street. This was the

Red Light District. In no other capital of Europe have I seen its equal. It was a street of Georgian houses and each one was a brothel. On the steps of every house women and girls dressed in everything from evening dress to a nightdress stood or sat. I was told that in the presbytery of the nearest Catholic Church was hung a map of the district and over Tyrone Street there was written in red ink, "No admittance even on business". An Irish lady has written a book to prove that Tyrone Street was a relic of the Crimean War. After that war two British regiments were quartered in Dublin and one old street directory showed that most of these houses were leased or owned by persons with foreign names, the camp followers. That may be so, but it was now Irish voices that invited the passing male to enter the House of the Harlot. When I told my father about Tyrone Street he made a memorable remark: "I would as soon sit on a barrel of gunpowder as go with a public woman." Another friend, Malcolm Watson, who was dramatic critic on the *Daily Telegraph*, London, said: "If you can't get it for nothing it's not worth having." Later I shall tell you how in 1926 this cesspool was cleared up by the Legion of Mary.

CHAPTER III

I Meet de Valera

My next visit to Dublin was in 1935 when on the evening of Sunday, 24th March, I lectured at the Gaiety Theatre in aid of the Dublin Catholic Library. The steamer from Liverpool arrived in the Liffey on the Saturday morning, and Mr. Erskine Childers came on board for breakfast. He became Postmaster-General in the de Valera Government. His father, who wrote that famous book *The Riddle of the Sands,* was shot by the Free State Government. After breakfast I went to the Gresham Hotel. Here at 10 a.m. Dr. Jim Magennis called to take me out for the day.

Dr. Jim Magennis was tall, broad-shouldered, clean-shaven, handsome, with a pleasant voice and charming manners. He was a physician to St. Vincent's Hospital and specialised in tuberculosis. He not only collapsed the affected lung by artificial pneumo-thorax, but also cut adhesions between the lung and the chest wall with the electric cautery. Most of us had left that to the surgeons. His consulting-rooms were at 70 Merrion Square where his father and brother Ned also practised medicine. Jim Magennis was devoted to his work and from him all patients, rich or poor, received the same kindness, skill, and attention. He was a great gymnast, especially on the parallel bars. He thought nothing of doing a hand-spring. He was the handsomest man in Dublin and many girls wanted to marry him. On one occasion an Irish millionaire called at 70 Merrion Square to offer his daughter's hand in marriage. Magennis replied that when he wanted to marry he was quite capable of proposing to the girl of his choice.

19

Our first visit was to the Plaza, then the headquarters of the Irish Hospital Sweepstake. The hall was gay with flags and Irish girls in costume. I saw the great wheels—one for the names of the horses, the other for the tickets to be drawn. I said all they needed now was a hospital ship to bring enough patients from England. The Hospital Sweep is perfectly fair, but remember when you buy a ticket the seller is under an obligation to send the money to Dublin and to show you the official receipt. Otherwise your number may not be included in the draw. At the Plaza I met one of the founders of the Hospital Sweep. He was Dick Duggan, the greatest book-maker in Ireland. We discussed the attempt of the Irish bookies to swindle the English bookies in 1920.

I had heard of this swindle from some Irish doctors who were employed at the Ministry of Pensions in London. They advised me that on a certain day I should back all the favourites at a small Irish meeting. At this meeting the Irish bookies would return every winner as favourite. Through their agents in England they had backed the favourites to win. I did not take part in the attempted swindle. Bookmakers and stockbrokers do their business on trust, and none of them had ever swindled me. Moreover I doubted if the swindle would work. Nor did it. The Irish overplayed their hand when a man whose usual bet was five shillings put £5 on every favourite, with doubles, trebles, and accumulators up and down. All the favourites won, and on paper those who backed them won a small fortune. But the swindle was too obvious and the offices refused to pay. They also cancelled the accounts of those who had participated.

Dick Duggan in reply reminded me of the greatest swindle ever attempted on the English turf. It was planned for an Easter Monday when there are many small meetings all over the country. During the previous week the sporting Press published the advertisement of a race meeting at a small town. The advertisement gave the races, the names of the horses, their weights, and the trainers. A reporter from the local paper wrote that if the sporting Press could not send a representative to the meeting he would telegraph the first three and their starting prices in each race for a fee of ten shillings per telegram. His offer was accepted. On the Monday night the street bookies paid out on the results as given in the evening papers. By Tuesday morning the offices had realised that this meeting had not been authorised by the Jockey Club. Further research showed that the names of the horses and trainers were fictitious. In fact there had been no race meeting.

Then Dick Duggan asked—"Will you be at Leopardstown this afternoon?"

"I hope so."

"Well, don't miss mine in the first race. I think it will win."

We were at Leopardstown and in the Members' Enclosure in good time. I put £2 on Duggan's horse in the first race. In fact I put the money on with Dick himself. The starting price was evens and the horse won. Then I said to Jimmy Magennis "I don't understand this. He tells us to back the horse. He keeps the price at evens and the horse wins. He must have lost a lot of money."

"This is a small meeting. The money he's lost here is nothing to what he has won in England where his agents have backed to win thousands at starting price. Here he's the leading bookie. As long as he lays evens none of the others can shorten the odds. That's why he kept up the price.

This began a good day's racing. Magennis knew most of the owners and trainers. Consequently we backed horses that were trying to win and several of them won. After every win we went to the Members' Club and drank champagne. Magennis told me of the horse he had in training. It was a present from a grateful patient and it had won the Irish

Cesarevitch. I asked him to let me know when he was backing the horse. Three months later in London I got a telegram that the horse was good for the three o'clock at the Curragh. The telegram also named a horse that was a fair chance for the four-thirty. I put £5 on each and lost £10. I had the consolation of knowing that Magennis had probably lost more.

After Leopardstown we motored back to 70 Merrion Square, where there was a tea-party with several very pretty women. There was also champagne for those who preferred that beverage. One woman told how her sister had written her in Irish which all the loyal Irish were expected to know. She could not read the letter, so she sent it to Miss Kathleen O'Connell, private secretary to Mr. de Valera. Miss O'Connell could not read the letter. So she showed it to de Valera. He could not understand the contents. Then the sister arrived unexpectedly. She had written to ask if she might come to Dublin for a week. She was told to write next time in English.

At 6.30 p.m. we all agreed to dine that night at Jammet's Restaurant. Then the drawing-room door opened and a tall man entered. The company became silent.

"Is Dr. Halliday Sutherland here?"

"Yes, I'm here."

"You were missing from your hotel this morning. I traced you to Leopardstown. So I supposed you would be with the Magennises. I suppose you have forgotten that at seven o'clock you are to dine at the University Club. I have a car outside. I shall drive you to the Gresham and then to the Club."

I bade my friends farewell and went away with the tall man. He was the Commissioner of Police for Dublin. In no other city in the world would such a thing have happened.

I spent a very pleasant evening at the University Club. There I met Professor Walter Starkie whom later on I knew in Madrid where he was Director of the British Institute. Being an Irishman he was and is the most popular Englishman in Spain.

On the Sunday evening Dr. Jim Magennis presided at my lecture in the Gaiety Theatre. I had written to the Committee of the Catholic Library that I would lecture on the Problems of Population. The Committee must have thought that this title was too dull, because they advertised the lecture as being "More Adventures at Home and Abroad". My first knowledge of the change was when I read it the previous day on the hoardings. It was then too late to prepare a new lecture. The new title attracted a large audience. Despite a tram strike every seat in the theatre was occupied.

The audience was enthusiastic, but the stage was most uncomfortable. It inclined downwards towards the footlights and standing for an hour on this inclined plane gave me cramps in the calves. I wondered how players could cross the stage without spraining their ankles. For half an hour I spoke on population. Then I read the script of my comedy *The Matchmaker*.[1] No reader had ever a more appreciative audience. They grasped every point of humour in this true story, and the whole theatre rocked with laughter. This was infectious and when blinded by my own tears of laughter I said, "If you don't stop laughing I can't go on reading." That brought the house down. After the lecture I went to a dressing-room where stewards brought in my books to be autographed. Every autograph brought 2s. 6d. to the Catholic Library. My fee for the lecture was £26 5s.

Jim Magennis motored me back to the Gresham Hotel. This was our last meeting. He died in 1940 at the age of 50. He died from overwork and emphysema. Emphysema is dilatation of the lungs, and this I think had been caused by gymnastics in middle life. He had a large practice and often visited patients after midnight. His health broke down at the

[1] Chapter IV of *In My Path*. 1936.

Final Examination in Medicine in 1940. He was one of the two Irish examiners in medicine. The external examiner was appointed by the Royal College of Physicians in London. After a morning's work the three examiners went to lunch at the Shelbourne Hotel. Here Magennis accused his Irish colleague of having been unfair to one of the students. Magennis became very excited. The external examiner, I think it was Dr. Langdon Brown, put his hand on the other Irishman's knee and said gently, "Take him home. It's Benzedrine." That was a brilliant diagnosis because in 1940 the toxic effects of Benzedrine, "the Happy Drug", were not well known. Magennis was taken to St. Vincent's Hospital. He died at 70 Merrion Square. His life was insured for £50,000. Magennis had never married. His father when dying had asked his two sons which of them would promise to look after their mother. Ned was already married, and Jim gave the promise...They are all dead now.

On the Monday forenoon Mr. de Valera, the Prime Minister, received me at the Government Buildings. I was there at 11 a.m. Four plain-clothes detectives guarded the foot of the staircase that led to the Prime Minister's rooms. Miss Kathleen O'Connell, his private secretary, was at the top of the staircase and I went up. She led me along a corridor and at the far end showed me into a room on the left-hand side. There was no one in the room. It was a large room with three doors. As I laid my hat and overcoat on the table I had the curious impression that I was being watched. On looking round I could see no place from which I might be observed. In any case it did not matter. I was unarmed. Miss O'Connell then opened the door and said, "I hope you will like our Prime Minister." She then opened a door on the other side of the corridor and announced me. As the door of this room clicked behind her I noticed that there was no handle on the inside.

Mr. de Valera gave me a very friendly reception. He

congratulated me on the lecture the previous night which he had been unable to attend. He asked if I represented any newspaper or if our talk was off the record. On hearing that our talk would be private he gave me an arm-chair where I sat facing him in the small room. He sat behind a desk which was in front of the wall next the door. Behind his chair was another door. This had a handle on the inside. These arrangements did not surprise me. At this time there were many fanatics in Ireland who believed they would serve their country by shooting de Valera.

He is a tall, lean, clean-shaven man with strong ascetic features. His serious expression was sometimes lit by a faint smile. At this time his Government was concerned about the activities of the I.R.A., the illegal Irish Republican Army. I remarked that one of the consequences of civil war was that some people thought every domestic difference should be settled by force.

"Well," said de Valera, "my arms are buried."

"I hope, sir, they are rusted."

He smiled and assured me he would never raise his hand against England. This I believed. He was always a brave and generous enemy. I wondered about the strange fate that had changed the Professor of Mathematics at Blackrock College into a great Irish stateman. His opponents say he is Jesuitical. To prove this they tell an amusing but apocryphal story of his boyhood in Ireland.

When he was ten he and another boy of the same age were once told to buy a loaf of bread after school and to bring it home. This they did, each carrying a loaf under his 'oxster'. We have that word in Scotland also. It means the space between the arm and the chest. As they walked home each began eating his loaf. As they neared home the other boy said, "We'll get into trouble for this." They walked on. Then he said, "I'll say you ate mine. You say I ate yours. Then we won't get into trouble."

"No," said de Valera, "we can't say that. It wouldn't be true."

They walked on. Then he said, "I know what to do. We'll change loaves."

That evening I returned to England.

CHAPTER IV

On Leopardstown Race-course

In the summer of the following year, 1936, I was invited to speak on a Sunday evening at the Drill Hall, Thurles, County Tipperary, on the Problems of Population. The steamer arrived at the Liffey on Sunday morning and I heard Mass at Adam and Eve's. That is what Dubliners call the Franciscan Church in Merchants' Quay. The Franciscans came to Ireland in the Penal Times when the practice of the Faith was forbidden by the English Government. The friars wore plain clothes and bought a public-house called the Adam and Eve on Merchants' Quay. In the cellars of the tavern, people could hear Mass and receive the Sacraments. So the church that now stands on the site of the public-house is known as Adam and Eve's. The Franciscans are much liked in Ireland. The people remember how they came.

There were no Sunday trains to Thurles but from Kingsbridge Station a train brought me to Roscrea at 12.30 p.m. There I was met by Dr. Esmonde who motored me across country to Thurles. He is now a T.D. or Member of the Dail. We stopped at one town for lunch and there I met the secretary of the association whose invitation I had accepted. At lunch Esmonde said, "Will you have Irish whiskey?"

"No, thanks. I don't like it."

"Well, you'd better get used to it. You'll get plenty tonight."

I had a bottle of beer. At 4 p.m. we reached Esmonde's house, and I asked for an hour to go over my notes. He put me in his consulting-room and said I would not be disturbed for an hour. A moment later he entered the room and set down on the desk a silver salver on which stood a full bottle of Scotch and a full bottle of Irish whiskey, a siphon, and a glass. I thanked him—"You forget that I've got to speak for an hour at eight o'clock."

"Well, it's there if you want it."

At five o'clock Esmonde returned. "Have you finished your speech?"

"Yes, thanks."

"Why don't you speak on Partition?"

"I haven't touched your whiskey but the air of this country is intoxicating. Yes, I will speak on Partition."

"Good, let's go."

We motored towards Thurles and on the outskirts of the town stopped at a cottage. We entered and found a man without his coat sitting at a table in a rather dark kitchen. He was introduced as the local reporter. Then Esmonde spoke: "Dr. Sutherland will speak on Partition at eight o'clock in the Drill Hall. He will dictate to you what he is going to say. When he has said it from the platform you will get the post-master to open the Post Office. You will then telephone what he said to Dublin."

The reporter lit a paraffin lamp on the mantelshelf, produced his note-book, and sat down at the table. Esmonde also sat at the table. I walked up and down the room while I dictated. On the sofa a boy of ten was asleep. He woke with a start and sat up. "It's all right, laddie," I said, "the Revolution has not yet begun."

At Thurles I was introduced to my host for the night, the Very Reverend Prebendary of the Cathedral. He was an old white-haired priest and very kind. At seven o'clock he gave a champagne dinner for the ten men who would form the platform party. Unfortunately before a speech my appetite for food and drink is diminished.

At eight o'clock we were facing an audience of a thousand

people in the Drill Hall. I first spoke about Partition. My theme was loyalty at a price. I reminded them of Lord Carson and Galloper Smith, afterwards the first Lord Birkenhead. They were so loyal that if George V had signed the Home Rule Act in 1914 they would have rebelled against their King. That was loyalty at a price. I recalled that during the Depression of 1932 an Ulster Member of Parliament had told the House of Commons that if the British Government did not order a cruiser to be built at Belfast they might throw in their lot with the South. That was loyalty at a price. The British people might end Partition if they knew what they were paying for the Parliament at Belfast. Ulster was smaller than Yorkshire, yet loyal Yorkshire was content with a County Council. If a majority of the people of Ulster wished to remain attached to England then let Ulster be made an English county and pay British taxes. If that were done they might decide to join the rest of Ireland. The way to perpetuate Partition was to continue maiming and killing innocent people with explosives left in English cloakrooms. England would never surrender to such cowardly propaganda.

That last statement was received in silence, and I knew I was speaking in the heart of the I.R.A. country. After the lecture I returned to the Prebendary's house. At 10 p.m. a priest arrived and asked if I could come to the hotel where many priests had gathered. They had been unable to hear my lecture and wished to meet me. I went and spent a very pleasant late evening.

I was wakened at 6 a.m. by men shouting and the noise of a farmyard in the street. On raising my blind I saw cattle, cows, and calves in the street and sidewalks. It was the Thurles Fair. I dressed and got breakfast at 7. The train for Dublin left at 8.30. I think the Prebendary was disappointed that I did not go to the Cathedral, which he said was very beautiful and only ten minutes' walk. But I was a stranger to the town. I made my way over dung-splattered pavements to the station. Some years previously they had tried to hold the Fair in fields outside the town. This had caused a riot because since the year dot the Fair had been held in the streets. On the way to the station I saw a bank that was open. I went in and found the floor covered with sawdust. At the counter the cashier shook hands and said, "A grand speech, doctor."

"So you were there?"

"Of course I was there."

"Your bank this morning looks more like a public-house."

"And if there was a bottle of stout in the safe you'd have it with pleasure."

"Will you cash a cheque?"

"Of course we'll cash a cheque."

"Have you English notes?"

"I'll give you every Englishman in the place."

He handed me twenty-six of the dirtiest £1 notes I had ever seen. This meant that the cattle-dealers also did business in Ulster.

I was in Dublin before lunch-time and went to the Gresham Hotel. On the steps I met Hughie, the hall porter. He remembered me from the previous year.

"A great speech, doctor. Ach, you're the talk of the town."

"Is it in the papers?"

"In all the papers except the *Irish Times*. You wouldn't expect to see it in that paper. Are ye for staying?"

"No, I go back to England tonight."

"Well, come in and I'll get you the papers."

I had lunch at the Gresham and read the papers. After lunch I telephoned Miss Kathleen O'Connell and asked her to tea at the Shelbourne. She agreed to meet me outside the Government Offices at four o'clock. I was sitting in the lounge when Hughie reappeared. "I've sent them away, sorr."

"Who did you send away?"

"Two reporters. You don't want to be seeing Protestant reporters from Belfast newspapers."

Hughie was a remarkable character and few who tipped him were aware that they were tipping a man much richer than themselves, for Hughie was reputed to own half the Gresham Hotel.

At four o'clock I met Miss O'Connell outside Government Buildings and we walked round to the Shelbourne Hotel. On the way she never mentioned my speech at Thurles. This surprised me because I expected a pat on the back from de Valera. Then she told me that they had been so busy that day they had not even seen the morning newspapers. At the Shelbourne we got a table. A man came in and sat at a table near us.

"That is Mr. Smyllie, editor of the *Irish Times*. Would you like to meet him?"

"Very much. Ask him over."

We were introduced and at once Mr. Smyllie said, "What the hell do you mean by coming here to talk politics?"

"Well, your paper had the distinction of being the only one that did not report me."

"Report you! I telephoned to Belfast what you said. . . . They can deal with you."

Miss O'Connell looked amazed and horrified. Then I laughed and said, "It's all right. We're both Scotsmen. We won't fight. You'll have tea with us, Mr. Smyllie?"

We had a pleasant tea.

Smyllie died in 1954. He was a great editor and was succeeded by Mr. Newman, who had been assistant editor. The *Irish Times*, despite its old associations with Dublin Castle and the English ascendency, is now regarded as the best of the Dublin dailies. It is certainly fearless. When an Ulster special constable shot an innocent motorist on the frontier in 1955, the other Dublin papers were confused. The *Irish*

Times put its finger on the point by asking if it was necessary for British soldiers, with arms and ammunition for their protection, to be protected by special constables?

Like most papers the *Irish Times* prints modern poetry much of which is quite unintelligible to me. In the old days when anyone talked nonsense we said he was a fool. Now we hail him as a genius, because we do not understand what he is saying. To rectify this perversion I suggest that papers should offer a prize for readers who can parse the printed poem. In my youth we were taught to parse poetry, that is, to put it into prose. This meant that at least we knew what it was about. I defy anyone to parse the following verse, quoted from memory, that appeared in the London *Tablet*.

> Four hands are on a Cross,
> Two are withdrawn,
> That leaves one,
> The Leopard howled.

After listening to two modern poets having an unscripted talk on the Third Programme of the B.B.C., I was moved to write the following appreciation:

All poets are young, but of the two overheard in the train one was younger than the other. I call them David and Jonathan.

DAVID: Our poetry does not sell.

JONATHAN: And that proves we are poets.

DAVID: Would it sell if we made it more intelligible?

JONATHAN: No, because at our best our words are unintelligible even to ourselves. Today some of our greatest scholars are seeking to discover what the poets of the nineteen-twenties had to say. So you and I must wait for at least thirty years.

DAVID: I promise to be patient for thirty years, but in the winter I am often cold and without a shilling for the gas fire. Could you lend me a few shillings?

JONATHAN: No, but our host for this week-end is a priceless mug. He has many possessions.

DAVID: May a poet steal?

JONATHAN: François Villon was a professional thief. Yet for one immortal verse he was kissed on the lips by a Queen of France. For his thefts he was sent to the galleys. You would be sent to Borstal. You would miss the romance of being chained to an oar. You would miss the sting of the overseer's whip on your sun-tanned shoulders. You would miss the tang of the salt spray on the open cuts. So do not steal but find a patron from whom you can borrow *ad lib.*

DAVID: You think a poet should have a patron?

JONATHAN: The more the better, provided we never hesitate to slander our generous donors and to bite the hand that feeds us.

DAVID: Maestro, you are magnificato!

JONATHAN: Sweet and pretty boy! We must join the B.B.C.

I am indebted to the Secretary of the Irish Jockey Club for a research that enables me to state that I spent Christmas 1936 with Dr. Harry Rutherford who owned a private Asylum, or as we should now say a Mental Home, at Finglas on the outskirts of Dublin. I arrived there on Christmas afternoon. Behind the Asylum was his stud farm. He had a magnificent stallion, five mares, and five foals. During the day the foals were in a field by themselves. They had all been born that year, and a foal takes its age from the 1st of January of the year in which it was born. Thus a foal born on 31st December becomes a year old on the following day. It is therefore advantageous in weight-for-age races for a foal to have been born early in the year.

Harry Rutherford had three brothers. All were doctors and we all had Christmas dinner at the house of the one who practised in Fitzwilliam Place, Dublin. He was married and had two daughters. Before dinner the younger girl changed into pyjamas and did a tap dance in the tiled hall to the strains of "You'll get a surprise" played by a gramophone. The guests stood along the walls. She danced very well. The dance finished opposite to where I stood. Then singing "You'll get a surprise" she kissed me and ran upstairs to change. At dinner I sat next her sister who seemed rather serious. Then suddenly she kissed me and stammered blushingly, "She bet me half a crown I wouldn't do it." It was a very pleasant dinner.

Next day Harry Rutherford motored me to the Members' Enclosure at Leopardstown Races where he introduced me to his friends. He told me it was usual to ask an owner or a trainer whom you knew about his horse. You expected him to tell you the truth. He himself had one unhappy experience. He was running a two-year-old for the first time to get the horse used to a race-course. He and the trainer thought so little of the horse that they did not employ a jockey. They allowed a young stable-boy to ride. Rutherford told all his friends that he had not put a shilling on the horse which could not win.

The race started and Rutherford was horrified to see his horse lead all the way and win by three lengths. He and the trainer immediately after the race had a word with the stable-boy. The trainer said, "When you get home you'll get the biggest thrashing you ever had in your life." The boy began to cry and Rutherford said, "Tell us the truth and perhaps you'll escape the thrashing." The boy stuttered— "It wasn't my fault. When I got to the weighing-in room all the Jocks said I couldn't win. I said I knew we couldn't win. So they said I could make the pace. They made me win, sir." The boy spoke the truth. Between the weighing-in room and the saddling enclosure these jockeys had managed to tell their friends to back Rutherford's horse on their behalf. It was a jockeys' race. An Epsom trainer tells me that this sometimes happens in England.

I was introduced to a very pretty woman and accompanied her as she gleaned information before each race. I heard her ask a well-known owner, "What about yours?" He looked at her for a moment and then replied, "I'd hate to see a pretty woman lose her money. Mine's got diabetes." Yet at that moment his horse had been made favourite. I shall name neither the owner nor the price. Let the punter remember that owners do not run horses for the benefit of the public. After every win we had champagne in the Members' Club.

After one such interval for refreshment I was late in rejoining my friends and the next race had started. It was a long steeplechase. They had backed Pride of Munster at 6 to 4, but the price now shortened to 5 to 4. They told me to walk down the line of bookies. There was a chance that one might call 6 to 4 because Pride of Munster was lying back. The bookies were behind the iron railing that separates the members from the next enclosure. It was a cold and windy day. My hat was well down and my overcoat collar was turned up. Dick Duggan was not there and none of the bookies knew me. I walked down the line. Suddenly a voice called out 6 to 4 Pride of Munster. I turned and shouted, "Who lays 6 to 4 Pride of Munster?" There was a moment of silence. Then all the bookies chanted, "Evens the field, evens the field." At that price I put on £2.

When I rejoined my friends, who stood on a small hillock facing the line of bookies, they were convulsed with laughter. "What's the joke?" I asked.

"How much did you put on?"

"Two pounds."

"It's the funniest thing that ever happened. You scared the ring. They thought you meant to lay hundreds."

Pride of Munster did not win. He was third, but the Irish Racing Calendar records the starting price was evens.

As we left the race-course to motor back to Dublin, Rutherford waved to a man in the rear car. "That's Colonel McCabe, the trainer," he said. Then I told him about Pukka Sahib. In 1921 my wife and I were living at Highgate, London, where the Passionists have a church at the top of Highgate Hill. The Rector was Father Malachy who told my wife that his second cousin had married Colonel McCabe. The Colonel had a horse Pukka Sahib that was entered for the Derby. On a time test in Ireland it had beaten all Derby records. So I put £10 on the horse at 20 to 1. The horse was unplaced in the Derby. Father Malachy told my wife the distance had been too short, and that Pukka Sahib would run in the Cesarevitch. Again I backed it. This time I put on £20 at 50 to 1, and stood to win £1,000. Two days before the race the horse was scratched. Catholics say you should never take a sweetheart or a servant on a priest's recommendation. To that I would add a horse.

We went for tea to the Shelbourne Hotel. There I was introduced to Miss B. Jameson the owner of Pride of Munster. She said, "I heard what you did at Leopardstown. Fortunately my money was already on. Had I been betting S.P. I would not have been amused."

On Sunday night at the Asylum I had a long talk with Rutherford about racing. "In England racing is the sport of Kings or millionaires but here in Ireland many doctors own race-horses."

"And there's no reason why you should not own a race-horse. If it wasn't unlucky I'd give you one of mine as a present, but you can buy the fastest of my foals."

"How would I know which was the fastest?"

"That's easy. Tomorrow morning after breakfast put a handful of lump sugar in your pocket. Go to the field and make friends with the foals. Give each a lump of sugar. Then when they know you, appear one day at the far end of the field. Hold out your hand and they'll come galloping to you.

Choose the one that gets to you first. Then come over to the yearling sales and buy the horse."

"What would it cost?"

"I won't bid against you. It should cost less than £100."

"And what then?"

"You take it back to England, enter it for the Derby, and have it trained."

"I can't afford the training."

"Of course you could. You have six children. All are at boarding-schools. A horse would not cost you more than a child. Besides, it will pay for itself. If it wins a couple of races as a two-year-old it has paid for itself. The Derby will give you something like twenty thousand pounds. But that's nothing to what you'll make out of stud fees."

At 2 a.m. I was very happy. I had won the Derby and was living in affluence on the stud fees. Next morning I slept late, and after breakfast I forgot to put a handful of lump sugar in my pocket.

In 1938 and 1939 I spent a few weeks each year at Murphy's Farm. This is on the top of a high cliff at Bray Head overlooking Dublin Bay. The farm belonged to Sergeant Murphy who had served in the Royal Irish Constabulary. It was a quiet place where I could write. Sergeant Murphy in the evenings over a turf fire told me many stories of the "Trouble" and of the Black and Tans. Once he had saved a village from being burnt and its people from massacre. The Black and Tans were stationed in his barracks. One evening they went out on leave and returned drunk. He had anticipated this and during their absence had put their guns and ammunition under lock and key. When the Black and Tans returned they wanted their guns. He told them they would get their guns in the morning when they were sober. He also locked the gates of the barracks and thus prevented them from getting out.

On another occasion Sergeant Murphy was with an English

officer in an open motor-coach filled with Black and Tans.
When they drove with speed through a wood the troops fired
into the bushes on either side of the road in case they con-
cealed an ambush. There was no ambush. The coach came
to open country and at slower speed passed through a small
town. There in the courtyard of the hotel Sergeant Murphy
saw Michael Collins on whose head the British Government
had put a price. Michael Collins turned and walked away
slowly. If he had run the troops would have shot him.
They always fired at people who ran. "I wondered if I should
tell the officer what I had seen. I did not tell him. In those
times it was difficult to get to confession. When I got to
confession I told the priest of my neglect of duty and he said,
'That's no sin. Your first duty is to your country and not to
a Foreign Power.'"

Early in 1939 I was returning by the night boat from
Dublin. In the smoking-room I saw a distinguished-looking
man sitting alone at a table. His white hair stood straight
out of his head. He was W. B. Yeats. I went and introduced myself. He gave me a friendly reception and invited
me to sit at his table. After some talk I said, "You may
think me rude but I would like to hear your scansion of
Innisfree."

"First I'd like to hear your scansion."

So I repeated these lines:

I will arise and go now, for always night and day
I hear lake water lapping with low sounds by the shore;

I added that the last line was one of the greatest onomato-
poeics in the English language.

He replied, "Your scansion is the same as mine." Then to
my great joy he repeated in a rich melodious voice the whole
poem.

He was a most pleasant companion and we arranged to
breakfast together on the train from Liverpool to London.

We went to our berths at 2.30 a.m.   Mr. Yeats was not on the train.   He was older than me.

My companion at breakfast was an interesting lady.   Her name was Miss Smith, and she had trained race-horses in India. She now had a riding-stable in England.   She told me Workman would win the Grand National and Blue Peter the Derby.

"You seem very certain."

"Well it's 4 to 1 against any horse getting round Aintree without falling.   Workman is the only horse in the race that has never fallen.   I've seen him run in Ireland.   Blue Peter is the best classic horse in England."

I told my wife of this tip and she advised me to back the double there and then.   I did not do so.   I backed the horses on the day of the races.   They won.   So did I, but I had missed a splendid double.   I know very little about racing but I could write a book on the mathematical flaws in every racing system ever invented.   I have bought that knowledge.

In 1953 I was invited to speak on any subject of my choosing in the Mansion House, Dublin, on Sunday, 11th October. The invitation was from the Committee of Vexilla Regis. This association, approved by ecclesiastic authority, consists of men who at the seminary found they had no vocation for the priesthood.   Such men are worthy of admiration.   The priest without a vocation has a life of misery and if he breaks his vows, especially the vow of chastity, may expect no mercy from the Catholic laity.   The aim of Vexilla Regis is to find employment for young men who have discovered in good time their lack of vocation for the priesthood.   This is a work of charity.   Too often the young man is abandoned by parents and ostracised by relatives.   They may have scrimped and saved to pay his fees.   They have got nothing for their money except a 'spoiled priest'.

The parents of a 'spoiled priest' have also lost in social

prestige. In Ireland the priesthood is so respected that some of the halo surrounds the family that produced a priest. The publican whose son is a priest is more respected than the publican whose son is a potman. The peasant family that includes a priest is superior to the common herd. How great is the prestige is illustrated in the following story told me by an Irish Catholic. He vouched for its truth. A widow kept a small shop in the village. Her only son was at the seminary. During examinations the widow spent much time in the back parlour where candles were lit in front of statues of the Sacred Heart, the Virgin, and St Bridget. She prayed that her son might pass. Sometimes her devotions were interrupted by the tinkle of the bell. Then she rose from her knees, went into the shop and sold short weight to the customer. Eventually her son passed his final examination. In the street the pious widow met a woman friend who said, "Congratulations that your son will be ordained a priest. Now you can spit in the faces of all your enemies."

The President of Vexilla Regis was the Assistant Commissioner of Police. I accepted their invitation with pleasure. I would speak on The New Spain, and asked them to invite the Spanish Ambassador. On the Saturday I went to Dublin by air and was met at the airfield by the committee and by Press photographers.

In the Gresham Hotel at eight o'clock a bell-boy called me and I found in the hall the Spanish Ambassador, the Marquis de Miraflores. He had been looking for me. "I have been to the Russell Hotel and then to the Hibernian, so I'm glad to find you here."

"Your Excellency, this is the first time an Ambassador has searched a city for me."

We went into the lounge and he spoke of the meeting on Sunday. "The Lord Mayor will speak after the Chairman because he has another meeting and must leave early. They have asked me to speak next. Do you mind if I do so at some length? I want to make a statement about our Treaty with the U.S.A.?"

"I shall be delighted."

"Then about Monday. That is Columbus Day, and if you are here the Embassy would like to give a cocktail-party in your honour."

"My grateful thanks. I shall certainly be here."

At this party I met the Marquesa. She was Andalusian, and I was flattered to find that she knew by heart portions of my *Spanish Journey*. I also met their four charming children all of whom attended schools in Dublin. In fact the eldest boy was the first person who could tell me that the Cursing Stones were on an island off Sligo. I also met some of the other ambassadors. The British Ambassador was not there.

The meeting on Sunday had also been successful. The floor of the large hall was filled but the gallery was empty. Before beginning my speech I stood aside from the microphone and asked, "Can you hear me at the back of the hall?" Some persons afflicted by deafness shouted "No". So I had to speak through the microphone. I think the microphone has done much to destroy the art of public speaking. It limits your movements and you cannot forget its existence. I have heard the greatest orator of my time, Lord Rosebery, Prime Minister of England. He had a golden voice and his whisper could be heard throughout the St. Andrew's Hall, Glasgow. He had no microphone. The hall in which I was now speaking had once heard the voice of Daniel O'Connell, the Irish Liberator. He had no microphone. In reply to the vote of thanks I told them a story of Daniel O'Connell.

On a visit to the U.S.A. O'Connell was addressing a great open-air meeting at Philadelphia. To this meeting had come a political opponent from Boston. He tried to interrupt the meeting by shouting "Louder, louder". O'Connell paid no attention until he reached his peroration which was as follows:

"And now, my fellow countrymen, I come to the end of what I fear has been a long and tedious speech [louder] to which you have listened with that courtesy [louder] and consideration you have always shown me, [louder, louder]. And as I gaze on this vast assembly I seem to see a still vaster assembly when on the Last Day the Recording Angel lays down the pen and the Book of Ages is closed. I hear the words in a voice of thunder—'Heaven and Earth shall pass away but My word shall not pass.' Then in the Infinite Silence, when a Universe shall meet its God, I hear the voice of a darned skunk from Boston yelling 'louder, louder'."

CHAPTER V

My Book is Banned

Mʏ book *Laws of Life* was commissioned in 1934 by the London publishers Sheed & Ward. It is a popular account of Love, Marriage, Divorce, Birth Control, Contraception, the Safe Period, The Law of Growth, Sterilisation of the Unfit, and Euthanasia. The first edition was published in November 1935. In the following year this was submitted to the Westminster Diocesan Board of Censors. The Board deleted nothing from the book, but required the addition of a few sentences to make clear the teaching of the Catholic Church on the use of the agenetic or safe period in marriage. On the 28th July, 1936, the book received the *Permissu Superiorum* from the Board. The second edition with the words *Permissu Superiorum* printed on the fly-leaf was published in November, 1936. This has been reprinted eleven times and to date over 80,000 copies have been sold. To booksellers this is known as a "bread and butter book".

The meaning of the words *Permissu Superiorum* (with the permission of the Superiors) is clearly stated in the following letter here published by kind permission of His Eminence the Cardinal Archbishop of Westminster:

ARCHBISHOP'S HOUSE,
WESTMINSTER,
LONDON, S.W.1.
14th March 1955.

Dᴇᴀʀ Dʀ. Sᴜᴛʜᴇʀʟᴀɴᴅ,
Thank you for your letter of 8th March.
If a book is to be passed by a member of the Ecclesiastical

Board of Censorship it means that there is nothing in this book contrary to faith and morals. Customarily, the Censor gives the Nihil Obstat, and if this is granted, the diocesan authority, i.e. Bishop or Vicar General, adds the Imprimatur.

Occasionally, it is judged that for one reason or another it is either unnecessary or undesirable that the publishers of the book should set out the full formula of censorship. This sometimes occurs with non-Catholic publishers, and in this case the diocesan authority may give permission for the words "cum permissu superiorum" to appear at the beginning or the end of the book instead of the Nihil Obstat and Imprimatur. The implication is, however, exactly the same.

As you say, the phrase "cum permissu superiorum" was originally intended for use in a case where a book had to be submitted also to a religious superior, but it is now used for books by clerics and laymen if the diocesan authority sees fit.

I trust this will answer your inquiries.

With a blessing and every good wish,

Yours devotedly in Christ,

B. CARD. GRIFFIN

Archbishop of Westminster.

Dr. Halliday Sutherland,
5 Stafford Terrace,
Kensington, W.8.

In Eire on the 10th October, 1941, the Minister of Justice, on the advice of his Board of Censors, banned the sale of *Laws of Life* on the grounds that this book was "indecent and obscene". Two things should be noted. In the first place the book had been on sale in Eire for about six years. Secondly it was revealed, as a subsequent debate in the Irish Senate showed, the Board of Censors had considered a copy of the first edition, although the second edition had been on sale for nearly five years. Consequently only the first edition was banned. I understand that this is now accepted by the Eire Customs and the second edition may be imported without let or hindrance.

On the other hand I have seen the letter from an Irish Bishop to the publishers in which His Lordship wrote, "In my opinion this book is indecent and obscene." He was referring no doubt to the first edition, but it passes my comprehension to know how a few words added at the behest of the Westminster Board of Censors could blot out all the indecency and obscenity in the first edition.

In 1926 the Government of Eire appointed a Commission to advise on Evil Literature. The Commission advised the banning of books, "written with a corrupt intent or aiming at corruption by reason of their appeal to sensual or corrupt instincts and passion". They urged discrimination between these and other books "having a purely literary aim in view but which as part of their reflection of the world admit representation of the vices or the passions that exist". The Commission's Report led to the Act for the Censorship of Publications which became law in 1929. Under this Act the Minister of Justice may ban the sale of any book condemned by the Board of Censors. This Board consists of five unpaid members who are appointed by the Minister of Justice. The Act was passed unanimously by the Dail. W. B. Yeats prophesied that it would become "an instrument of intellectual tyranny". In 1946 the Government of Eire set out an Appeal Board under the chairmanship of a Judge of the High Court. To this Board authors and publishers whose works had been banned could appeal.

In Britain the law is:

First. The publication of any "Obscene libel" is a misdemeanour punishable at common law.

Second. By the Obscene Publications Act of 1857 power is given to seize obscene publications before they are distributed.

Chief Lord Justice Cockburn said in 1868: "The test of obscenity is this—'whether the tendency of the matter charged as obscenity is to deprave and corrupt those whose minds are open to such immoral influences and into whose hands a publication of this sort may fall.'"

Lord Cooper, the Lord Justice General in the High Court of Justiciary in Scotland said in 1952: "The book or picture itself provides the best evidence of its own indecency or obscenity or the absence of such qualities."

Referring to this opinion, Lord Chief Justice Goddard in the Court of Criminal Appeal in 1954 said: "This Court desires to adopt every word of it."

In Britain it is a misdemeanour to publish an "obscene libel". This is defined in Lord Campbell's Act of 1857 and applies "exclusively to these works written for the single purpose of the corruption of youth". The publisher of such a book may be indicted before a Jury at Quarter Sessions, the Assizes or High Court, and if found guilty is liable to imprisonment and / or a fine. Here it may be doubted if an ordinary jury are competent to decide the issue. Thus a jury whose reading matter included a Sunday newspaper devoted to crime and sex might overlook everything except the most blatant pornography. In any case this method of censorship is unsuited to Eire where the majority of books are imported from Britain and U.S.A.; consequently the publishers of those imported books are beyond the jurisdiction of the Irish Courts.

The police in England and Wales may ask the local magistrates to authorise them to seize and destroy any copies of a book offered for sale in the locality provided that the magistrates agree that the book is an obscene libel. This method of censorship is unsatisfactory because a book that is banned in one town may be on sale in the next. Thus in 1954 the Swindon magistrates ordered Boccaccio's *Decameron* to be destroyed, although the book could be bought in Oxford and London. The bookseller appealed to the Quarter Sessions who quashed the order to have the book destroyed. Moreover the B.B.C. announced the reading of twelve chapters from *The Decameron* on the Third Programme. I heard three chapters. In fairness to the Swindon magistrates I think these chapters had been edited. Not that I think *The Decameron* comes under Lord Campbell's definition of obscenity. It was written to entertain, although some children and adolescents will find indecency in its pages as they would in those of the Old Testament. Moreover *The Decameron* contains the most beautiful story of children's innocence. Two of a French king's children, a boy and a girl stood in front of a picture of Adam and Eve. "But which is Adam and which is Eve?" said the boy. "Stupid", retorted his sister. "You can't tell until they put their clothes on."

The Senate of Eire in 1942 had a long debate about the Board of Censorship. Sir John Keane moved a vote of censure on the Board. He cited three books which in his opinion had been banned without cause. Two were books by Irish authors, the third was *Laws of Life*. The debate began on 18th November and lasted four days. The Official Report runs to over 84,000 words. From this Report I quote the following excerpts. They throw light on the psychology of Ireland or in plain English on how Irishmen think.

SIR JOHN KEANE: "I move:

"That, in the opinion of Seanad Eireann, the Censorship of Publications Board appointed by the Minister for Justice under the Censorship of Publications Act, 1929, has ceased to retain public confidence, and that steps should be taken by the Minister to reconstitute the board. . . .

"I have got one other book—I shall refer to several in passing—to which I wish to refer. Here again I approach the matter with hesitation but I cannot help it. This is a book called the *Laws of Life*, by Halliday Sutherland. I want to be as clear as I can about this matter. It is difficult to get exact information nowadays on account of postal delays and one thing or another of that kind, but my information on the best

47

authority is that the book is issued *permissu superiorum*. That is not the *imprimatur*, but I understand that the only difference between it and the *imprimatur* is the difference between a first-class and a second-class ticket. I may be asked whether the edition I have got is the one that is issued *permissu superiorum*. My answer is that all editions of the book have been banned and the only grounds on which they have been banned are that the book deals with the question of the safe period. Now I am not going into the question of the safe period, but I do claim that the knowledge and use of the safe period is approved by the Catholic Church. I should like to hear on what grounds, other than the reference to the safe period, this book has been banned. I say that advocacy of the safe period does not bring the book within the definition of a book which advocates unnatural methods or unnatural prevention of conception. I do not want to elaborate this matter, but I say that the safe period is not, to my mind, unnatural, and I leave it at that. . . ."

MR. BOLAND:

"The other book—the *Laws of Life*—is more a medical book, and I read that book, too. Senator Sir John Keane was kind enough to let me know what three books he intended to deal with in this debate. He selected these because, I suppose, they would provide the Censorship Board with their weakest case. I read that book before it was banned and I could see that it was a medical book. It advocated, as Senator Sir John Keane said, the use of the safe period, as it is called. I am satisfied that, if that book were in general circulation in this country, it would do untold damage. The *permissu superiorum* to which reference has been made may exist in England because conditions there are different from conditions here. Birth control is, I believe, freely advocated there. Whether it is widely practised or not, I do not know. The free advocacy of birth control is not allowed here, and I think the Censorship Board were bound to recommend the banning of the book. I have no apology to make for the Board."

PROFESSOR MAGENNIS:

"Thank you very much. I was dealing with the reiterated charge against the Censorship Board, that it had horrified the public with the enormity of its offence, that it had banned an indecent—more frequently than not the remark was 'banned on the grounds of indecency'—a book which had been approved by the Cardinal Archbishop of Westminster— occasionally there was substituted 'the Westminster Synod'. Here, it was said, was a Catholic author, a man of eminence in England, known as the Catholic champion against birth control, and his book was published by an eminent Catholic firm, and these fools and asses, these men who, in eloquent language of Mr. Sean O'Faolain to the *Irish Times*, made 'fools of themselves and an ass of the Minister'—or 'a fool of the Minister and asses of themselves'—in condemning it. Now, that went through practically every newspaper in Ireland. I could produce, if required, cuttings to show no fewer than five of them from one source—'Our Correspondent from Dublin.' Unless that were rebutted, unless that were taken in detail and refuted, the board undoubtedly would lie under a pall of misunderstanding, followed by condemnation from all the people who have read these criticisms. I am saying that by way of an apology beforehand for being rather long. It is a matter of detail, and detail is always tedious except in competent hands.

"I have said already, in my previous statement, that we did not ban a book, on the grounds of indecency, which bore the *imprimatur* of the Cardinal Archbishop of Westminster or of any other Bishop.

"I have already exhibited the book to the Chair and to the House, to show that the work sent in with the complaint has no *imprimatur* of any Bishop, no *nihil obstat* of any censor, no

49

permissu superiorum, no formula of any kind indicative of Church approval. Not only that, but on the title page of the book there is no indication that it is by a medical man or that it is a medical work. It is a collection of essays. As a matter of fact, some of them are exceedingly interesting. The title is *Laws of Life*, by Halliday Sutherland, published by Sheed & Ward, 1935. I have said that, at the time that this complaint was submitted to the board, there were, in point of fact, a second edition and later impressions of the second edition. As inquiry reveals, this second edition and the further impressions of it, do bear the words '*Permissu superiorum*, 28th July 1936', over the inscription 'first published, November, 1935'.

"The book was not condemned as indecent, or, as Deputy Dillon, in the passages I read out, said, 'on the grounds of indecency'. It was banned for indecency within the meaning of the Act—a very important difference, as I hope to show. The Title of the Act under which we are appointed, and under which we work, and to the terms of which we adhere with the utmost strictness is: 'An Act to make provision for the prohibition of the sale and distribution of unwholesome literature'. The charge has been made repeatedly that we defy the Act and disregard its requirements. Why, there would be less to be said against us if we were not so rigorously compliant with the terms of the Act. The policy of the Government, of which Mr. Cosgrave was President, and the policy of the present Government that succeeded it, is to protect the people of this State from the influx of 'unwholesome literature'. . . .

". . . *Laws of Life*, in large measure a medical book, of extreme value to the medical practitioner and to priests as confessors, that is, priests hearing confessions in the confessional. A book written for them, containing valuable scientific knowledge for them, can be in existence and available for them only if printed and published. It consequently may be printed and published without coming under the danger of an indictment as giving publicity to obscene literature. If the House will be patient with me, I will read this again, because it is a very vital part of our case: 'The circumstances of publication may also be of importance'. . . .

"It is in that connection that the passage I read from *Laws of Life* about London in 1910 and London in 1942 with its streets denuded at night of the usual street walkers, because of the extended operations of the amateur, is valuable. To what factor does he attribute the rise and prevalence of the amateur practitioner? To the indiscriminate circulation of knowledge about birth control. But then, I can show you that his own book circulated just as might a book on how to spot a winner or as some handbook teaching how to win the victory in bridge, might be published, is indiscriminate circulation of teaching about birth control and teaching injudiciously, erroneously. . . .

"Having studied very carefully the *Laws of Life*, we saw at once that the book might have peculiar value for a limited class of readers, and anyone who reads it will see that it is because that it is so the author was at pains to write it and get it printed and published. We saw also the risk there was of its falling into improper hands, of its having an undesirable circulation. He, himself, in express words, points out that the circulation, without safeguards or without precautions, of knowledge about methods of limitation of families, is one of the causes of the replacement of the professional by the amateur. . . .

"Let me come now to the book, the banning of which involves this terrible thing that shocked the heart and conscience of Frank O'Connor and Sean O'Faolain and their associates. The monstrous enormity of banning a book that had the *imprimatur* of an Archbishop! When they first made that charge, they thought they would get away with it. They had eventually to add, like the hot water to the Oxo, a little diluting matter, and then it became a book that had the

sanction of a board under the Archbishop of Westminster. It
is pretty much like the story of the three black crows. They
found that there was a second edition—and even the second
edition did not bear an *imprimatur*; it had, as I read already,
the words *permissu superiorum*—and then they proceeded to
slang us with renewed vigour. We banned the book on the
grounds of indecency—I have dealt with that already. We
banned the book that had the *permissu superiorum*.

"They never thought of going into the second edition and
comparing it with the first, but I did, and this is where, in the
popular phrase, they lose their horse. The very points in the
original book on which I fastened when we were examining it
as a board of censorship are the very points that, in order to get
the *permissu superiorum*, have had to be omitted or re-worded.
I wonder what Senator Sir John Keane will say to that, he who
made such repeated play with the *imprimatur*. Here is one of
the statements in the original book—I can quote it from
memory, but, if the House prefers, I will read it. It is on page
36, and this is the original book we had before us:

(*The Senator quotes.*)

"You will observe that he is not the champion of anti-
birth control: he is an advocate of birth control. What he
objects to is the other fellow's method of limitation of families.

"Now this is the important point. What I fastened on in
the book was what purported to be a statement of Catholic
doctrine with regard to certain periods of infertility. . . .

Engaged couples, under the economic pressure, who cannot
afford to marry, and yet unable to resist the carnal urge, might
be tempted to use this. This first edition, providing calcu-
lation as to how to determine the infertile periods becomes
what I called it at the time we were reporting to the Minister—
the fornicator's *vade-mecum* or, if you like, the harlot's handbook. That is what it would become if circulated indiscrimi-
nately published with those words—that 'the Catholic Church

permits the use of the safe period'. I have finished with this book, thank Heaven, so far as reading from it is concerned."

DR. ROWLETTE:

"The next speaker was Senator O'Buachalla, and he puzzled me because he seemed to my simple mind to be rather contradictory in his outlook. He said: 'Senator Keane's standards are not ours.' That is irrelevant, but the suggestion behind it is that we have a higher standard in this country than other people have or than the unfortunate Senator Sir John Keane has. We have had a great deal in this debate of what I thought was unnecessary, irritating and futile—this pharisaical attitude that lies behind a statement of that kind: we are not as this poor publican. Senator after Senator made statements which were modern renderings of the ancient statement: I thank thee, O God, that I am not like others and not like this poor publican. Whether it is true or not that we are not like the poor publican, or like the debased people who live outside the four shores of this country, it is an unhealthy attitude for any reasonable man to adopt that he is better than another. We all hope that we are better than other people, or we try to be better than other people, but I think we make a great mistake to plume ourselves on it as was done publicly by several members during the last day's debate. . . ."

PROFESSOR TIERNEY:

". . . Another point that I dislike about the whole debate on this unfortunate book is the tendency to debate it from the standpoint that on our side is virtue and Erin and on the other side the Saxon and guilt, or something of that sort. There is a tendency to throw a white sheet over ourselves and pretend that we are the purest, finest, most lovely people in the world. . . .

"The other case is that much discussed case of the *Laws of Life*, and we are all very indebted to Senator Magennis for the long account that he gave of the circumstances that led to its banning. Having listened to him with great attention and respect, I still cannot agree that it was wise on the part of the Minister to accept the advice of the Censorship Board and to ban the book. I quite admit the copy that was banned did not bear the *permissu superiorum* and that there was a definite misunderstanding about that, and I am naturally prepared to concede to Senator Magennis the point he made as to the changes between the two issues. None the less, the fact remains that for our Irish Censorship Board and our Government to censor, as in its general tendency indecent and obscene, a book published by one of the best known and most respected Catholic publishing firms in the world, and published, no matter in what circumstances, with the *permissu superiorum* of the Westminster Archdiocese, was certain to raise some scandal and to give rise to grave doubts in the minds of many people, not only in the minds of people whose profession in life is the writing of obscene literature or any kind of literature, but in the minds of ordinary Christian people, especially of Catholics both here and in other countries. Though we may have our own peculiar standard of virtue—as is so often asserted in this debate—we are not so immune from the whole wide world as that we can afford lightly to indulge in actions like that and not expect to suffer for those actions.

"I am inclined to believe as one citizen, sincerely I hope, and not prejudiced on the question, that by banning a book like that we ran the risk of incurring far more evil results, both at home and abroad, than we would by leaving the book alone, whatever be its merits or demerits. While on that point, I would like to say, in reply to Senator Magennis, that it is a book that not only has been consulted by confessors, but has been recommended by confessors to their penitents. When we find ourselves banning a book like that, there is something wrong, something that is not going to be very conducive to our reputation in the world. It is because

of that that so many people, not people of one particular type
or class of religion, are concerned about the matter. . . ."

SIR JOHN KEANE:

"I think the effect of having these things discussed freely
and frankly is on the whole healthy. That is my reply to
those who say standards do not change. Right and wrong
remain the same, but certainly reticence and talk and frank
discussion do change. That is the only point I want to be
clear about. Then another Senator said that there is no
demand for these books. If there is no demand what of pre-
venting their circulation? There must be a demand for them.
One Senator said that the *Laws of Life* was selling like hot cakes,
and that shows that some people do want to read it. It was
also said that world standards are not our standards. That has
been the subject of correspondence in the Press and I do not
propose to go into it. I do not say that we are any worse than
others, but I do not think we are necessarily immeasurably
better. I think we have got our weaknesses. We have all
got different standards, but when I come to think of things I do
see things that are open to criticism. I do not think our
standards of illegitimate birth or even infanticide are anything
to be proud of, and I do not think our State-licensed betting
shops, where temptation is thrown in the path of people
every day, are anything to be proud of. I am prepared to
say that they do more harm than literature. If I was asked
whether I choose between the pre-censorship position and the
present I would certainly say eliminate the betting shops and
let the pre-censorship position with regard to books and
literature continue.

"I now pass to the *Laws of Life*. I do not think the Senator
in his defence of the banning of that book was altogether
happy. He gave a very long explanation of it, but the facts
are perfectly simple. I admit that the board did not know,
at the time that they banned this edition of the book, that a

later edition had the *permissu superiorum*. I cannot help feeling that if the board had known that they would not have banned the book. That may be so, but here is a book that had the *permissu superiorum* of the Catholic Diocese of Westminster and which—unless I am contradicted—I can say is allowed to circulate freely among Catholics outside this country. I think at one time that the Senator said indirectly: 'Why should the board not exercise its independent judgment?'—but I do not think the board stand on that. However, the fact remains that the book has the *permissu superiorum* and the board do not deny that it circulates freely among Catholics. Apparently then, they say it is not desirable that it should circulate freely among our people here. This is the book which the Senator said should only be put into the hands of students or confessors. By what authority do they say that? There is nothing in the Act to bear that out.

"Under the Act books can only be banned for two reasons. One is that they are in their general tendency indecent and the other is that they advocate unnatural methods of contraception. It has not been suggested, I think, that this book is in its general tendency indecent. Let us see what the Minister says in regard to this book. I think his is a much more frank statement of the case than we had from the Senator.

"The Minister said:

"With regard to the *Laws of Life*, whether the board was technically and legally correct, whether the book was in its general tendency indecent may be open to question, but on the ground that it was calculated to do untold harm I am perfectly satisfied that it should be banned."

"I like that type of honest statement, but what is the legal authority for this? The Minister is not entitled, nor are the board entitled to say that because they are of the opinion that a book will do harm it should be banned in consequence. That book is not in its general tendency indecent, nor does it advocate unnatural means of contraception. It advocates the use of the safe period, and I am informed that on occasions the Catholic Church allows the use of the safe period.

"I was hoping that the Senator would have thought better of what he said when he saw the record, but I am afraid he has not. I cannot help feeling that he will be sorry when he sees himself on the record as saying that this book which had the *permissu superiorum* of the Catholic authorities in England and which, I contend, should not have been banned within the Act is, as he said, 'the fornicator's *vade-mecum* or, if you like, the harlot's handbook'. Surely there is no necessity to be dirty, because that is dirty, and he said it of a book approved by the Catholic Diocese of Westminster which circulates freely among Catholics in England."

Results of the Debate:
For the motion   2
Against the motion   34

I first heard of this debate from a lady doctor in London who telephoned—

"Have you seen what Professor Magennis has said about you in Eire?"

"No."

"He says you will be known as the author of the Forni-cator's *Vade-Mecum* or the Harlot's Handbook. What are you going to do about it?"

"When next in Dublin I shall call on Professor Magennis, and I'll lay even money that he asks me to dinner."

Unfortunately Professor Magennis was dead by the time I next went to Dublin. My immediate reaction to the debate was to send the following letter to the *Irish Times,* the *Irish Press,* and the *Irish Independent.* All three published my letter on 18th December, 1942. The *Irish Times* gave it banner headlines on the front page.

With reference to the Senate debate on censorship, reported in your issue of 3/12/42, I, one of the banned authors from beyond the pale, crave permission to make the following statements.

In the first place, I agree with Senator Magennis that the *Permissu Superiorum* only means that a book is not inaccurate in its references to Catholic Doctrine. The first edition of *Laws of Life* (Nov. 1935) contained several statements contrary to Catholic Doctrine; and these were corrected in 1936 edition, which received *Permissu Superiorum* of Westminster. In that edition certain biological errors to which Professor L. P. H. Renouf, of Cork, had very kindly drawn my attention, were corrected.

Nevertheless, I do not agree with Senator Magennis that these corrections made the 1936 *Laws of Life* "practically a new book". They obviously make it a better book; but I do not follow how this makes a relevant argument for maintaining the ban; unless the new book is as bad as the old, in which case the reference to corrections is irrelevant. Indeed, at the back of my mind, I have the idea that this book has been banned for the wrong reasons.

Finally, I recognise that any Sovereign State has the right to ban what books it will and as Senator Magennis has challenged the banned writers to test the charge of bad faith against the Board of Censorship in the Courts rather than in the Senate. I now declare that so far from having made a charge of bad faith against anyone concerned in this matter, I have never, either directly or indirectly made any objection to the ban on *Laws of Life*. Nor have I authorised any objection to be made directly or indirectly, by the publishers.

I do not believe that Laws of Life was banned for the chapter on the Safe Period. A larger book *Control of Life* was published in September 1944. This book has two chapters on the Safe Period. It also received the *Imprimatur* from the Westminster Diocesan Board of Censorship. The publishers, Messrs. Burns, Oates, & Washbourne, London, publishers to the Holy See, were excused from printing the ecclesiastical approval. Nevertheless this book was not banned in Eire where the fifth edition is now selling.

I believe *Laws of Life* was banned because I had written in the cold language of physiology an account of the function of sex. This could harm no one from the age of puberty upwards. In Eire too many people, including clerics, regard ignorance as synonymous with innocence. These persons should inquire how many Children of Mary from Eire are now prostitutes in Piccadilly.

CHAPTER VI

At a Trappist Abbey

IN 1955 after a week in Dublin I went on 15th April to Mount Saint Joseph Abbey, two miles from Roscrea in the County of Tipperary. The abbey is a Trappist monastery. Every Trappist is a Cistercian and every Cistercian is a Benedictine, but not every Benedictine is a Cistercian or a Trappist. The Cistercian branch of the Benedictine Order was founded in 1098 by Abbot Robert from the Benedictine monastery of Molesme in France. He and twenty monks left the monastery in order to practise the Rule of St. Benedict more strictly. They went to the forest of Citeaux, fifteen miles north of Dijon and settled there. The Romans had named the place Cistercium. Hence the new community were known as Cistercians.

Thirty young noblemen came to Citeaux in 1112 and were admitted as novices. Their leader was Bernard who later became the Abbot of Clairvaux where he had 700 monks. Of him Gibbon wrote: "In speech, in writing, in action, Bernard stood high above his rivals and contemporaries. He became the oracle of Europe."

Bishop Malachy, of Armagh, stopped at Clairvaux when making a visit to Pope Innocent II in Rome. He was so impressed by Bernard's monastery that he asked the Pope for permission to relinquish his diocese and spend the rest of his life as a Cistercian at Clairvaux Abbey. The Pope refused permission, but permitted him to leave four of his companions at the abbey to be trained as Cistercians. These four accompanied by some of St. Bernard's monks came to Ireland and founded Mellifont Abbey in 1142. Soon this abbey had so many monks they were able to open fresh foundations and by the year 1200 there were 26 Cistercian abbeys in Ireland. Bishop Malachy had died on a visit to Clairvaux and was later canonised. His head and that of St. Bernard are enclosed in the High Altar of the Cathedral at Troyes.

The late Dr. Healy,[1] Archbishop of Tuam has told what these Cistercians did for medieval Ireland: "There is one essential element in the constitution of the Cistercian monasteries which, I think, ought to commend itself to us all. The Cistercian monks, as a rule, lived by the labour of their own hands. . . . Every member of the community should work—*laborare est orare*—was their maxim. Work done for the community was in itself a prayer. Their tasks were different—but all had to work, and even the abbot, peer of Parliament though he might be, if he was true to his rule, was expected to work some time in the garden or the field. It was good for his own health and good for the example it gave the community. . . .

"Irish agriculture, such as it is, owes much to the Cistercians. They reclaimed and manured the land; they raised abundant crops; they made their fields the greenest and most fertile in the whole country. They are still to be seen—those fertile fields—now in the hands of the stranger, often-times reclaimed from the brake and morass by the unceasing labour of the monks. The Celts were not great agriculturists; they were a pastoral people. The Cistercians were their best teachers in showing how to till the soil extensively and successfully. . . . The monastery was, by its labour, a self-supporting institution, which made the most of all the natural resources at its disposal, for the benefit, not only of the inmates of the house, but of the whole surrounding community. The monks fed themselves and the poor on the produce of the crops planted, reaped and dressed by themselves. They

[1] See Dr. Healy's *Papers and Addresses,* published by C.T.S., Ireland.

clothed themselves with the wool of their own flocks, shorn, spun, woven and sewn by themselves. They built their own monasteries and churches, for amongst the brethren were architects, masons, carpenters, painters—men in fact of every craft, who were as a rule members of the community. . . . Then all these laboured for God; it was not for money but for God they did their work, and hence they did it so thoroughly, so grandly, so beautifully, that their labour in those far-off days still puts to shame even the greatest achievements of our boasted civilisation. . . .

"Moreover the abbey had its own school for the younger members of the community. . . . The youth of the neighbourhood were also admitted to these monastic schools, and received such education as they needed. . . . Many of the monks were highly skilled in the medical science of the time, and gave the benefit of their advice not only to their own brethren, but to the sick of the neighbourhood, to whom both medicine and medical advice were freely and gratuitously dispensed whenever it was needed. . . . The technical shops had masters to teach all mechanical arts—and above all, horticulture in the garden, and agriculture in the fields.

"So . . . when you see a monastery like this in its ruins, it commands our respect, not only because it was once the sanctuary of religion, the home of self-denying men, but also because it was the school, the dispensary, the hospital and the alms-house, for the poor of all the country round about it."

Then came the suppression of the monasteries by Henry VIII, whose Commissioners reported about the Cistercians in Ireland that they were "notoriously given up to idolatry and the pestiferous doctrine of the Roman Pontiff". The Cistercians were suppressed and their lands and possessions confiscated to the Crown. Under Elizabeth I many of the monks suffered martyrdom. At Mainister, near Limerick, on the eve of the feast of the Assumption, August 14th, 1585,

forty monks were beheaded in the church before the Blessed
Sacrament. At Graiguenamanagh, Co. Kilkenny, twelve
monks went out to meet the soldiers of Elizabeth and refused
to obey the Queen's command. They were slaughtered
where they stood. Thus the Cistercians were driven out of
Ireland.

The Cistercians returned to Ireland in 1831. In that year
64 Irishmen and six Englishmen from the monastery of
Mount Melleray in Brittany landed at Queenstown. By 1833
they had founded what became the Abbey of Mount Melleray
on the rocky Waterford hills. The Irish Cistercians adopted
the strict observance of the monastery of La Grande Trappe in
France. Hence the name Trappists. In 1876 Count Moore of
Mooresfort, Co. Tipperary, gave the Cistercians a large estate
near Roscrea. Here in 1878 they founded what is now
Mount St. Joseph Abbey. Hither I was bound.

From the main road a private drive of a quarter of a mile
leads to the guest-house. To the left beyond tennis courts and
playing-fields is the domestic Gothic of Mount St. Joseph
School. This was built in 1905 and houses 270 boys. It is
one of the best known boarding-schools in Ireland and the fees
are only £100 per annum. Again to the left is the church.
Behind this is the monastery, the monks' garden, and the farmyard. Then at the top of a slight eminence overlooking the
church is the guest-house. This was once an old castle of
which two lateral circular towers remain. Between the towers
the guest-house had been built.

On the ground floor to the right of the entrance, was the
ladies' dining-room. Women visitors sleep outside the
grounds in a house on the main road but come to the guest-
house for meals. On the left of the entrance was the door of
the men's guest-house. A Brother unlocked the door and
let me enter. You could always open the door from the
inside, but from outside you needed the Brother with the key.
The dining-room table could seat 40 people and was covered

by a single woven Irish linen tablecloth, the largest I ever saw. On the first and second floors were the bedrooms. Mine was at the top of the house. Breakfast was at 8 a.m., dinner at 1 p.m., and supper at 6 p.m.

The guests were friendly people and the first I met was a journalist from Dublin. He told me an amazing story of a village in Tipperary. In this village the priest preached in Latin, and outside the church the entire congregation and their children spoke in Latin. The shopkeepers and the whole village spoke in Latin. I asked the whereabouts of this village. "It's an easy motor run from here." "The name?" "Well the village is called Lattin." This shows how your leg may be pulled at a Trappist guest-house.

I also met a young man in the uniform of an Irish Army recruit. He was 16 and had come here, with a recommendation from a Dublin priest, to offer himself as a novice to the monastery. He told me the abbot that morning had interviewed him to find out if he had the necessary qualifications to be admitted to the novitiate as a postulant, and he continued, "If they accept me as a novice they will send me to Dublin University."

"Have you got the leaving certificate?"

"No."

Even if he had the leaving certificate it was most improbable that the Trappists would send a novice to the University. He also told me: "In the Irish Army discipline is stricter than in any other army in the world except the German Army."

"Well, the German Army no longer exists. How many men are in the Irish Army?"

"Four million."

"Good. Then Ireland can tackle Russia single-handed."

Next day he was gone, and a Brother told me the young man had returned to Dublin.

A farmer with three of his friends had motored from Ulster. Of all Catholics in Ireland, so a Brother told me, those from Ulster were the best. The farmer was aged 66 and he had had an interesting life. "My father died when I was 20. He and my grandfather had been drunkards. It was not their fault. They just couldn't help it, but they drank the farm. That's why I've never touched the stuff. I'm afraid it might get hold of me. So I migrated to the U.S.A. and got work delivering goods in the haulage department of a Chicago railway station. Do you know I prefer to work for an Englishman or an American. They're fair. But if you work for an Irishman and get up against him he'll never forget it. My boss in Chicago was a Mason, a very high-up Mason. He knew I was a Catholic, but was very good to me. Then came World War I. Being a British citizen I was conscripted into the American Army. I was nineteen months in France. I was once in hospital with neuritis in my right leg. Then we went back to the States where I received an honourable discharge. After that I became a naturalised American citizen. Then I met my wife, an Irish girl, and we returned to Ulster where I got a small farm. A year ago I met an Irishman who had also served with the American Army. He noticed my occasional limp and asked how old I was. I said 65, and he told me I should apply for a pension. I thought this was nonsense, but I wrote to the American Embassy in London. Lo and behold I was called before a medical board at Belfast. It was a British Ministry of Pensions Board and I was examined by a Naval doctor. He reported to the Embassy. Since then I've been drawing a pension of £28 a month. I sometimes wonder what is my nationality because I vote at elections in Ulster."

At the guest-house we were awakened at 6 a.m. and heard Low Mass in the public church at 6.30. The public church is that part of the abbey church nearest the guest-house. A wooden partition separates the public church from the abbey church. At 7 a.m. a Brother opened a gate in the partition and we entered the abbey church to hear High Mass. In the late afternoon you may hear vespers and compline. At 7 p.m. we retired to our rooms.

One afternoon a Brother showed me over the monastery. Next the church is a large sacristy. Here I saw vestments of pure silk. The silk threads are spun on the estate and the vestments are woven in Dublin. Beyond the cloisters is a good library. Then I saw the refectory. Here silence prevails. The monk who drops a teaspoon or clatters a plate must then rise and prostrate himself on the floor before the Lord Abbot. After a moment or so the Lord Abbot knocks on the table, then the offender may rise and return to his place. The monks and Lay Brothers serve in turn at table. A monk may not ask anything for himself from a Brother, but he may draw the Brother's attention if his neighbour lacks anything. An apocryphal story is told of the monk who found a dead mouse in his soup. He paused for a moment. Then he beckoned the Brother and said in signs, "My neighbour has no mouse in his soup."

The Trappists are vegetarians. Meat, fish and eggs are forbidden, but butter, and milk foods, rice, vegetables and roots are allowed. For the Trappists Lent begins on the 14th September and lasts until Easter. During this period they are allowed six ounces of bread in the morning and two in the evening with a little jam. For drink they have tea or coffee in the morning and tea or cocoa in the evening.

For dinner two cooked portions are allowed. If soup is given it counts as a portion; dessert is added every day except on fasts of the Church and Fridays. For dessert raw or cooked fruit are given but never cheese. A typical dinner is vegetable soup, potatoes and cabbage or other vegetables and dessert. From Easter to the 14th September they are allowed six ounces of bread and butter in the morning with a further six ounces of bread and butter in the evening with dessert or salad. The Trappists usually live to a ripe old age and among them cancer is very rare.

The community numbered 120. There were 42 priests, 12 novices, 20 scholastics, and 46 lay Brothers.

At the top of the monastery is a large dormitory with 120 beds. Each bed is within a small cubicle made of curtains on rails. The beds are entirely of wood, and on the slats is a straw mattress and pillow with sheets and blankets. The entire community sleep here, except the Lord Abbot. He has a similar bed, but a room to himself. I asked the Brother about snoring. "Everyone snores," he said. "When I get to bed I try to get to sleep before it starts. When you've been looking after someone who is sick in the Infirmary and get late to bed, then you know how people snore."

The time-table for the monks is—

a.m.

2.0	Rise. Little Office of the Blessed Virgin Mary.
2.30	Mental Prayer.
3.0	Canonical Office followed by private Masses and thanksgiving.
5.30	Office of Prime after which we retire to the Chapter Room where a chapter of the Holy Rule of Saint Benedict is read and explained by the Lord Abbot. The beds are then made before our first meal which is called mixt.
7.30	Office of Tierce and High Mass.
9.0	Manual Labour.
11.30	Office of Sext.
12.0	Dinner followed by interval during which monks devote themselves to study, spiritual reading and private prayer.

p.m.

2.0	Manual Labour.
4.15	Vespers and Mental Prayer.
5.30	Supper.
6.0	Spiritual Reading in common.

6.30   Compline.
7.0   Retire.

For the Lay Brothers the time-table is—

a.m.
2.0   Rise, followed by office in church.
3.0   Work.
4.0   Assist at Masses.
5.15   Breakfast, followed by work.
7.45   Tierce, Sext at place of work, followed immediately
        by work.
10.45   None, Spiritual Reading.
11.30   Dinner.   Clearing tables, etc., followed by Spiritual
        Reading.

p.m.
1.0   Work.
4.45   Vespers at place of work.
5.0   End of work.   Interval.
5.30   Tea (or supper).   Washing up, etc.
6.10   Reading in Community.   Compline in the church.
7.0   Repose.

On Sundays they follow the same routine as the choir
monks.

Theirs is a hard life but these Monks and Brothers are content.   To the sybarite who hankers after the flesh-pots of
Egypt, a skinful of drink or the gratification of a nerve,
their life is lunacy.   They are worshipping God, the Supreme
Spirit who made everything out of nothing.   Nothing is
something beyond comprehension.   We do not even know
what is substance.   They say all matter is made of electrons
revolving round a proton as the planets revolve round the sun,
but the electrons are revolving millions of times a second.
We do not know what electrons are.   Yet they make it easy

to think of the universe as a thought in the mind of God. If He ceased to think of it, it would vanish into the nothing whence it came. We do not even know what electricity is, or magnetism. They say the universe is expanding like a balloon being inflated. Expanding into what? We cannot comprehend space without end, or eternity which has neither an end nor a beginning. We are very ignorant.

They say we have evolved from a primordial living cell spontaneously generated in the sea at the time when the world was young. How it happened no one knows, but it never happened again. The genes of this primordial cell had the potentiality of forming the vegetable and animal kingdoms. From this cell came everything that ever lived on sea or land, from a scrap of seaweed to the forest giant, from dinosaurs to viruses. A virus is a cell so small that it cannot be seen by the microscope. It causes disease in plants and animals. A virus cannot have been the primordial cell because it lives on the cells of higher organisms. Thus evolution has produced all living things, large and small. This is as marvellous as anything in the first chapter of Genesis. The B.B.C. are now plugging evolution into school-children. No doubt they think this knowledge will reduce juvenile delinquency.

Unfortunately evolution is an unproved theory. It is not supported by the fossil record from the rocks. In the earliest or igneous rocks, which were once molten, there are no fossils. A Canadian once said he had found in these rocks a fossil of the Dawn Animal. This caused a ten-day newspaper sensation, until someone pointed out that a similar fossil could be seen on any earthenware plate that had been many times in the kitchen oven. The simplest fossils are found in the earliest chalk deposits. Then as one geological period succeeds another fossils of more complete animals are found in each successive strata of rocks. Thus in sandstone, laid down twenty million years ago in the U.S.A., are the fossils of herrings. These are identical with the herrings that now swim in the North Sea. In Europe fossils have been found of every animal now living there. The same will probably apply to other continents when their geological strata have been fully explored. The fossil record shows no missing links. There is no fossil intermediate between a fish and a snake, nor any between a snake and a bird. As G. K. Chesterton said, the only thing about the Missing Link is that it is still missing. The last Missing Link has been found to be a fake. This was the Piltdown skull discovered some forty years ago. In 1954 experts proved that this was a genuine fossil skull of a pre-historic man. To this skull the jaw-bone of a modern ape had been fitted. The fake was discovered by scientists at the Natural History Museum, South Kensington, London. It is interesting to note that they received several abusive letters from persons who must have been very proud of their simian ancestry. Creation is an unsolvable mystery. From memory I quote Thomas Carlyle: "Though man stands in the centre of immensities and in the conflux of eternities he may say of the Universe 'This is my home', such power is in the words well spoken *Credo*, I believe."

The guest master showed me over Mount St. Joseph School. It was vacation and the boys were not there. I saw the spacious class-rooms, some well equipped for the teaching of chemistry and of physics. The kitchen was all electric. To the Brother in charge I remarked that this must have been expensive. He replied: "It has saved us a lot. The slaughter-house have telephoned to ask if we were starving the boys, because we were taking one instead of two bullocks a week. The boys have as much meat as they want, but all the cooked meat is mechanically sliced. This means less waste, and on that we saved a bullock a week."

In the school museum on the first floor landing is a stuffed specimen of the Mouse Deer. This extraordinary animal is fourteen inches long and a foot high, and resembles a minia-

ture deer. The card attached to the exhibit says: "Chevrotains, or mouse deer, forming the family of Tragulidae, are so
like small antlerless deer in appearance, that they are com-
monly regarded as nearly allied to the musk deer, near which
they were once placed by naturalists, but when examined
anatomically they are found to depart widely from the deer
family. Chevrotains agree with the true ruminants in the
absence of incisor teeth in the upper jaw and resemble the
musk deer in the presence of upper tusks, or canine teeth
which in the males attain a considerable length and project
below the upper lip. They also agree with true ruminants
in that the canine teeth of the lower jaw resemble the incisors,
to the outermost pair of which they are approximated so as to
form a continuous series. The three molar teeth and the last
premolar tooth in the upper jaw, together with the lower
molars are also of a crescent-like type, but with that the
resemblance to the true ruminant ceases."

Fr. Austin, the curator of the museum, is not certain whether
the 'deer' in the museum is a Chevrotain or not. The
gentleman who owned it called it a mouse deer. It came
from Siam, where the natives rear them as house pets.

One afternoon I walked half a mile through the grounds to
the abbey flour-mill beside the road to Roscrea. The mill
grinds wheat for the monastery and for farmers within a radius
of thirty miles. The Brother in charge of the mill told me that
between here and Roscrea I could see six derelict mills, which
showed how fertile once the country was. At the mill the
wheat is ground as in ancient days between the upper and
nether millstones. The mill is powered by a water-turbine
on which the water falls from a height of twelve feet. The
wheat is ground into whole-meal. The wheat berry consists
of a shell or bran which contains the germ. The rest of the
shell is filled with the endosperm. Here is an analysis of the
various components:

	Endo-sperm.	Bran.	Germ.	Whole Wheat.
Water . .	13·0	12·5	12·5	14·5
Proteins . .	10·5	17·0	35·5	11·0
Fat . . .	1·0	3·5	13·0	1·5
Starch & sugar .	74·0	43·0	30·5	69·0
Cellulose & fibre	1·0	18·0	3·0	2·5
Mineral matter .	·5	6·0	5·5	1·5
	100·0	100·0	100·0	100·0

This explains why Irish bread is so good.

In England most of the wheat is ground in steel roller mills which throw out the husks and the germ. The white flour millers call these valuable constituents 'offal'. This is fed to animals. The germ is also made into expensive proprietary medicines, so that the public may buy what they should have had in their bread. Only the endosperm is ground into flour, and even this flour is treated with chemicals.

Flour is bleached by nitrogen peroxide gas or by the addition of benzoyl peroxide powder. Flour is "improved" for baking by addition of one or other of the following chemicals—ammonium persulphate, potassium persulphate, potassium bromate, and acid calcium phosphate.

Certain gases have the property both of bleaching and 'improving' flour, these being chlorine gas, beta gas, a mixture of chlorine and nitrosyl chloride, addage gas (chlorine dioxide) and agene gas (nitrogen trichloride).

With the millers of Britain agene gas used to be the most popular, and until recently a large percentage of the flour sold in the United Kingdom was 'agenised'.

White flour is deficient in vitamins and nutrient salts. If that were all, it would be bad enough, but there is now evidence that 'agenised' flour contains a substance that is poisonous for dogs.

The disease known as Canine Hysteria, 'running fits', or 'fright disease', has been observed for the past twenty years or more in Britain and the U.S.A.

Many veterinary surgeons had attributed this disease to ticks, worms, or to the after effècts of distemper. In 1931 Melnick and Cowgill discovered that dogs developed hysteria if fed on a diet including gliadin, the alcohol-soluble fraction of wheat protein. Therefore dog-biscuits and meals manufactured at high temperatures came under suspicion. Yet the problem was not yet solved because the disease might be due (a) to the lack of some nutrient property, or (b) to the presence of some toxin in the bread.

Sir Edward Mellanby's experiments have now solved the problem. Dogs from the same litter were fed on a balanced diet of milk powder; peanut oil; lean meat; baker's yeast; ascorbic acid; salt; vitamins A and D; and a cereal.

The cereal was cooked by steam for 90 minutes at low pressure (0·5 lb.).

On this diet the dogs grew up healthy provided the cereal was untreated, 'unimproved', flour or oatmeal. If 'agenised' flour—the flour out of which 90 per cent of the bread of the British people is baked—if that flour was used the result was hysteria.

When staying at a Trappist or indeed at any monastery you are not charged for board and lodging, but on departure you make an offering. An American millionaire did not believe this. He was a Protestant, and when in Ireland he went to Mount Melleray, the largest of the four Trappist monasteries in Ireland. He stayed for three weeks and was never asked to pay. Nor was he asked to pay on his departure. He sent a large donation to the monastery.

Both Mount Melleray and Mount St. Joseph were favourite retreats for alcoholics. A Sligo solicitor told me of one of his clients who took to drink. The first symptom was frequent visits to the solicitor's office where he, an elderly man, tried to make love to the girl clerks. Then one morning he would be found in his pyjamas at the top of a lamp-post. His friends got him home, dressed him, and drove him in a motor-car to Mount St. Joseph. Here they handed him over to the guest master. On the return journey they stopped for lunch at the hotel at Roscrea. After lunch they went into the bar to have a drink. Seated at the bar and drinking whisky was their friend. He had escaped and walked the two miles to the hotel. . . . They took him back to the monastery.

I asked the guest master about the alcoholics. He said they still admitted some of their old customers, but any new cases were sent to a nursing home. There they pay twenty guineas a week. "That's a grand cure. It's not fair to other visitors to have alcoholics about the House. I noticed that many visitors never write from here. I suppose they fear their friends might misunderstand why they were here."

Before leaving Mount St. Joseph, I met the abbot, who, when he heard that I was writing on my visit to the abbey, asked me to correct two popular widespread myths about the Trappists.

The first is that Trappists are vowed to silence. They are not vowed to silence. Within the monastery there is a strict rule of silence. As every Catholic knows there is a difference between a vow and a rule. It is one thing to break a rule, but much more serious to break a vow, because a vow has been made to God. Moreover those whose duty means dealing with the general public are dispensed from the Rule of Silence. Thus the Father and Brothers who look after the public in the guest-house may talk to their heart's content, and are usually excellent conversationalists. Again a few Trappists who form a small community in a parish where they are doing parochial work are dispensed from the Rule of Silence.

The second myth is that every Trappist digs his own grave. I am authorised by the Lord Abbot of Mount St. Joseph to say that no Trappist has ever been ordered, or even allowed, to dig his own grave.

"Here," said the Lord Abbot, "our community numbers 120, but you imagine the state of these grounds if everyone was allowed to dig his own grave."

The place would certainly be a death-trap on a dark night. There is one peculiarity about the burial of a Trappist: he has no coffin. He is fully dressed in boots, stockings, shirt, and the habit consisting of the robe, the scapular, and the cowl with a hood drawn over the head. Thus he is laid in the grave and covered with earth. Coffins were not in general use until the sixteenth century. Our Lord had no coffin although He was buried in the sepulchre of a rich man, Joseph of Arimathea.

Before leaving Ireland, I paid a brief visit to Mount Melleray in the Knockmealdown Mountains. One author who lived there for eight days has recorded that he saw open graves and was told that these had been dug by Trappists. I saw no open graves. The guest master took me into the garden. No open graves were visible. He said the author in question may have seen holes for the foundation of the Abbey Church and that some one had pulled his leg.

In my youth a similar story was told about the Poor Clares, an order of Franciscan nuns. Many of my generation will remember a painting, widely reproduced, called "The Vale of Rest".

I have forgotten the name of the artist but it showed two Franciscan nuns digging a grave. The sight of two beautiful women dressed in the Franciscan habit and engaged in this mournful task must have brought a tear to the eyes of millions who did not know that the subject of the picture was sentimental bunkum.

CHAPTER VII

The Magdalen Home

From the Trappist Abbey of Saint Joseph a fellow guest motored me to the City of Galway. Here I was an honorary member of the Galway County Club which overlooks the grass square in the centre of the town. It is a residential club and from the members I received much kindness and hospitality. The honorary secretary Mr. H. St. J. Blake, a solicitor, left the next day to attend a meeting of the Knights of Malta in Rome, but I had tea and dinner with his wife and family. Their home was three miles out of town and was next the home once owned by the late Professor Morris. When Mrs. Blake learnt that I wished to visit the Children's Home at Tuam she telephoned Dr. Walsh the Archbishop who gave permission and also invited us to tea at Archbishop's Palace. Next day Mrs. Blake and her son, a law student at Galway University, motored me to Tuam some twenty-five miles distant. Far to the left of the road is a Faery Hill round which at night phantom horses race.

At Tuam I went to the old workhouse now the Children's Home, a long two-storied building in its own grounds. These were well kept and had many flower-beds. The Home is run by the Sisters of Bon Secours of Paris and the Reverand Mother showed me round. Each of the sisters is a fully-trained nurse and midwife. Some are also trained children's nurses. An unmarried girl may come here to have her baby. She agrees to stay in the Home for one year. During this time she looks after her baby and assists the nuns in domestic work. She is unpaid. At the end of a year she may leave. She may take her baby with her or leave the baby at the Home in the hope that it will be adopted. The nuns keep the child until the age of seven, when it is sent to an Industrial School. There were 51 confinements in 1954 and the nuns now looked after 120 children. For each child or mother in the Home the County Council pays £1 per week. That is a pittance. If a girl has two confinements at the Home she is sent at the end of the year to the Magdalen Home Laundry at Galway. Children of five and over attend the local school. All the babies were in cots and the Reverend Mother said, "We wouldn't allow a girl to take her baby to bed with her unless it was at least two months old. Then she is probably fond of it. Before then there might be accidents." The whole building was fresh and clean.

In the garden at the back of the Home children were singing. I walked along the path and was mobbed by over a score of the younger children. They said nothing but each struggled to shake my hand. Their hands were clean and cool. Then I realised that to these children I was a potential adopter who might take some boy or girl away to a real home. It was pathetic. Finally I said, "Children, I'm not holding a reception." They stopped struggling and looked at me. Then a nun told them to stand on the lawn and sing me a song in Irish. This they did very sweetly. At the Dogs' Home, Battersea, every dog barks at the visitor in the hope that it will be taken away.

Mrs. Blake, her son, and I had tea at the Archbishop's Palace where Dr. Walsh gave us a very friendly reception. His Grace had recently been to England where arrangements had been made for a hundred Irish priests to visit England every year and give Missions to the Irish emigrants. The English branches of the Legion of Mary would visit the Irish Catholics who did not go to church and would try to induce them to attend the Mission. In this way it was hoped to check the leakage of Irish Catholics from the Church in England.

Back at the Galway County Club I asked the assistant

manageress how I could visit the Magdalen Home. She told me I would need permission from the Mother Superior of the Convent of Mercy but that before I could see the Mother Superior I would need to see the Bishop of Galway, the Most Reverend Michael John Browne. In Ireland every Bishop is the Most Reverend to distinguish them from the Protestant Bishops who are the Right Reverends. She telephoned the Bishop's secretary and I was given an appointment for the following morning.

Next morning Colonel Stacpoole, a member of the club, drove me to the Bishop's Palace where at 11 a.m. I was received by the Most Reverend Dr. Michael John Browne. He is tall, well built, with blue eyes, strong features, and iron-grey hair. Our conversation was as follows:

BISHOP: So you're writing a book about Ireland?

MYSELF: I hope so.

BISHOP: Well, if you write anything wrong it will come back on you. Remember that.

MYSELF: I have said it's impossible for anyone to write about Ireland without getting into trouble.

BISHOP: As you drove here, did you see the Bird's Nest at the corner of the road?

MYSELF: No, my Lord.

BISHOP: Do you know what a Bird's Nest is?

MYSELF: No, my Lord.

BISHOP: There you are. Trying to write about Ireland without knowing our background.

MYSELF: I'm willing to learn.

BISHOP: At the time of the Famine (1845) the women who lived in the Bird's Nest bought Irish infants from their starving mothers for five shillings each, and brought them up as Protestants.

MYSELF: Why so?

BISHOP: To provide Protestant servants for the large Protestant houses. Then there were the Misses Plunkett, two

Protestant ladies who bought an estate in Galway. They ordered the tenants to send their children to the Protestant school. Those who refused were evicted. That meant death by starvation.

MYSELF: Damnable.

BISHOP: It would be good if you wrote about the Birds' Nests. There are some in Dublin.

MYSELF: I will, if I hear about them.

BISHOP: You've only to ask.

MYSELF: I'm surprised that Protestants should still be so keen on their religion.

BISHOP: They've plenty of money.

This I knew, for when Gladstone disestablished the Church in Ireland in 1870 they received two million sterling as compensation. I also knew that the Bishop had offered them £80,000 for the return of the Church of St. Nicolas in Galway. This church seats 2,000, but the offer was refused although the present congregation numbers not more than 70 persons.

MYSELF: My Lord, I would like to see the Magdalen Home Laundry.

BISHOP: Are you going to write it up?

MYSELF: Until I see it I don't know whether there is anything to write about.

BISHOP: I am their Bishop. It is my duty to defend these nuns. I have done so in the past and shall do so again.

MYSELF: Is there anything to hide?

BISHOP: No, there is nothing to hide.

MYSELF: Are the girls paid?

BISHOP: No, they are not paid. By their work they pay for their board. I suppose that offends your Welfare State principles.

MYSELF: Some of us think that England has gone too far with the Welfare State.

BISHOP: Why do you want to see the Magdalen Home?

MYSELF: I want to see how you treat unmarried mothers. Many of these girls come to England. It is said that fifty-five per cent of the girls in British Catholic Rescue Homes are Irish.

BISHOP: That is propaganda. Father Craven began it. Cardinal Bourne repeated it. For twenty-five years I have asked for the figures. They can't give them. Do you know the figures?

MYSELF: No, I'm trying to get them.

BISHOP: You will find there are only a few. Hundreds of decent Irish girls are going to England. At this moment your Government are advertising high salaries for Irish girls to go to England as nurses in your mental hospitals.

MYSELF: English priests say that most of the Irish lose their Faith within six months of coming to England.

BISHOP: Then why don't your English priests look after the Irish instead of throwing bastards in our face?

MYSELF: My Lord, no one is throwing bastards in your face. Ireland is a Christian country where going to Mass is a social duty difficult to avoid.

BISHOP: That is normal. It should be so in England.

MYSELF: England is a pagan country. Only one in ten of the population has any church connection. In England it is easy to miss Mass. Are the girls at the Magdalen Home free?

BISHOP: Yes, they may leave if their parents or some other person will be responsible for them. Last year a man took out a girl. She was his deceased wife's stepsister. He took her to England where a priest married them. Of course the marriage was invalid.

MYSELF: Why so?

BISHOP: Deceased wife's sister. That requires a Dispensation.

I did not ask whether this applied to a deceased wife's stepsister. I am told that it does. Nor did I suggest that the English priest might have obtained a Dispensation.

BISHOP: Are you prepared to submit anything you propose to write about the Magdalen Home for approval by the Mother Superior of the Sisters of Mercy?
MYSELF: I am, my Lord.
BISHOP: Then I permit you to go there.
MYSELF: Thank you, my Lord. Years ago I said that there could be no peace between our two countries until England remembers and Ireland forgets. I am tired of meeting Irishmen in London who speak as though Cromwell had left Ireland the day before yesterday.
BISHOP: Forget? Did you ask the Spaniards to forget? No, because they would not have listened to you. We are not commanded to forget but to forgive. I like your books, but your theology is all wrong.
MYSELF: And I thought every Scotsman was a born theologian.

The Bishop made no reply. So I kissed his ring and said farewell.

Colonel Stacpoole who had waited for me outside the Bishop's Palace now drove me to the Convent of the Sisters of Mercy where I was to see the Mother Superior. Her predecessor was Mother Mary Macdiarmaid, who came of a county family. Of her an Irishman said to me—"She was a grand girl. She used to thrash the inmates of the Magdalen Home, but they loved her." The present Mother Superior received me with every courtesy and arranged to meet me at the Magdalen Home at five o'clock that afternoon.

At five o'clock I was at the Magdalen Home and was introduced by the Mother Superior of the Convent of Mercy to the Sister-in-charge and six nuns who managed the laundry. We were all seated in the Sisters' parlour where I put my questions. Most were answered by the Sister-in-charge.

"How many girls have you?"

"Seventy-three."

"How many are unmarried mothers?"

"About seventy per cent."

"And the others?"

"Some are sent here when they leave the Industrial School because they need special care."

"Are they mental defectives?"

"No."

"Backward?"

"Yes."

"Are the girls paid?"

"No, they earn their keep."

"This imposed labour must mean a large profit to the Magdalen Home."

"No, these girls do not work like other girls. If a girl gets tired of working in the laundry we do not force her to work. The Home is self-supporting. At present we are overdrawn at the bank and shall be so for two years. The new chapel and the recreation hall cost a lot. Also this year we hope to give the girls a more attractive uniform. On Sundays they're allowed to use cosmetics."

"Are the girls free?"

"Yes."

"Can a girl leave whenever she chooses?"

MOTHER SUPERIOR: No, we're not as lenient as all that. The girl must have a suitable place to go.

"Last week one girl made such a row that we let her go. That night she was ringing the bell and begging to be re-admitted."

"If a girl ran away, I suppose the Guards could easily find her?"

"The Guards are not very helpful because the girls are free."

"What about discipline?"

"We give them a good scolding when they need it."

"And more serious offences?"

"We stop their food."

"For how long?"

"Only one meal and we know that the other girls feed them."

"And more serious offences?"

"These are rare. One girl threw her shoe into a washing machine and broke it. We had the expense of a man coming from London and his stay at the hotel."

A NUN: It's wonderful how they respond to kindness. They take offence about things the ordinary person would think of as nothing. But they're grateful for any little kindness.

"How long do they stay?"

"Some stay for life. Most of them are Consecrated Penitents. Every year there is a service when they may be consecrated. They are much respected by the others. When they die they are buried with the nuns. The others are buried in the common burial ground."

I was then shown over most of the Home. There was a beautiful Chapel and a splendid Recreation Hall. The latter had a polished floor on which the girls could dance, a stage with cinema screen and a projector. The last film shown had been *The Song of Bernadette*. A nun told me the girls preferred religious to secular films. In a room upstairs I saw many of the girls. A small elderly woman had a small black cape round her shoulders and from the front of the cape hung a large crucifix. She was a Consecrated Penitent. I asked her how long she had been here.

"Twenty-five years."

"Are you happy?"

"Yes, very happy"—and she smiled.

Next I spoke to a young girl. She had been here for three

months. She did not look like an unmarried mother. So I risked the question: "What brought you here?"

"I didn't get on well at home. I lived with my brother. Then he married."

"And you didn't hit it off with your sister-in-law?"

"Oh, she's all right."

A nun told me that later the girl said to her, "I couldn't tell him I'd been in an asylum."

The next girl to whom I spoke wore what looked like a fancy waistcoat with brass buttons over her uniform.

"How long have you been here?"

"Six months."

"Do you like it?"

"Yes." But this girl never looked me in the face, and a nun later said to me, "She is a bold girl."

Before I left the Magdalen Home, the nuns offered me an excellent tea.

I shall now try to answer the question put to me by the Most Reverend Michael John Browne, Bishop of Galway. In plain English the question is: How many unmarried Catholic girls from Eire have babies in England? Below are figures from the Crusade of Rescue in the Diocese of Westminster, which includes the County of London north of the Thames, Middlesex and Hertfordshire. The figures show the number of unmarried Catholic girls who sought help for themselves and for their unborn children in the years 1950 to 1953.

The Catholic Children's Welfare Council whose headquarters are at Coleshill near Birmingham, have all the figures about unmarried Catholic mothers in England and Wales. As the Catholic laity subscribe to these societies, I think we are entitled to have all the figures. Nothing is to be gained by a policy of hush-hush. If the Irish in Britain knew how much was being done for their unfortunate fellow countrywomen they would subscribe generously to the charities.

The Magdalen Home

	1950	1951	1952	1953	*Totals.*
Number of girls pregnant from Ireland . . .	84	121	111	79	485
Number of applications from Irish girls . .	382	509	213	489	1,693
Number of applications from English girls . .	60	131	162	141	494
Number of applications from Foreigners . .	85	151	304	81	621
Total number of applications	611	912	790	790	3,291
County of Origin					
Dublin . . .	102	214	143	98	557
Tipperary . . .	16	28	40	64	148
Kerry . . .	42	78	62	92	274
Kildare . . .	9	37	29	84	179
Wexford . . .	9	36	34	55	134
Waterford . . .	11	37	44	45	137
Clare . . .	9	34	20	40	103
Meath . . .	10	35	30	36	111
Roscommon . .	8	18	14	12	122
Donegal . . .	6	4	12	5	27
Cork . . .	152	272	212	149	785
Limerick . . .	3	2	4	7	16
Sligo . . .	3	4	11	8	26
Kilkenny . . .	5	86	48	31	170
Offaly . . .	2	4	8	11	25
Galway . . .	8	11	13	19	51
Mayo . . .	11	47	21	28	107
Cavan . . .	4	8	14	13	39
Longford . . .	23	27	14	20	94
Louth . . .	4	8	7	18	37
Monaghan . . .	9	14	10	12	45
					1,693

These figures refer to the unmarried Irish girls who applied for help to the Westminster Crusade of Rescue.

In these four years of 3,291 applications, 1,693 or 50 per cent were from Irish girls. Of these 485 or 28 per cent had become pregnant in Eire. These girls resist any suggestion that they should return to Eire for their confinement. They say that in Eire the unmarried girl who wishes her baby to be adopted has to stay for one or two years, without pay, in a Catholic institution.

There are two Magdalen Homes in Dublin, at Gloucester Street, and St. Mary's, Donnybrook. Girls may leave these Catholic Homes at will but efforts are made to retain them when possible. Regarding Protestant Homes there is Mrs. Smyllie's Home, known as the Bird's Nest at 19–20, York Road, Dun Laoghaire, and there is also the Irish Church Mission at No. 5, Townsend Street, Dublin. At 112–116 Orwell Road, Rathgar, there is The Bethany Home, open to girls in distress.

The proselytising influence of these homes has been largely negatived by the Home of the Legion of Mary—Regina Coeli—which caters for prostitutes and unmarried mothers irrespective of religion.

In England, some Irish girls come direct from Euston Station to the Crusade of Rescue. In some cases the Irish Catholic priest, to whom the girl told of her condition, gave her five pounds and the following advice: "Go to England for your confinement. Leave your baby there to be adopted and return to Eire." That is charity because in Eire the girl who is known to have had an illegitimate child is the prey of every rascal in the parish. But this charity is done at the expense of English Catholics.

The Westminster Crusade of Rescue is a charitable society founded in 1859 and incorporated in 1905. In December 1955 *St. Peter's Net,* the official magazine of the Westminster Crusade of Rescue, published the following statements:

"We have also had news of the project which will result in many Irish priests coming here to try and help their people become integrated into parish life here. The English secular press has also commented on the problems and some of them, daily and weekly, have treated the matter very prominently. The tendency has been to overstress the numbers who find themselves in moral danger and we have heard of angry and puzzled Catholics who cannot reconcile some of the more unpleasant allegations with what they know of the Irish people they meet at Church and parish activities and whose children mix with their own in the parochial schools.

"As the name of the Crusade of Rescue has been used in this connection, we feel obliged to say something to put the problem in its right perspective. Much comment has been ill-informed and there is no doubt that an unhealthy curiosity has prompted a lot of the publicity. On the other hand we cannot pretend that we are not very anxious or that we are able to deny the allegations. The truth is that we are so harassed by the problems of the unmarried mother and her child, and have been for many years, that we are almost glad that at last we are in a position to speak out. We had to wait until Irishmen, and especially Irish priests, spoke first.

"The Crusade of Rescue has, for many years, devoted a major part of its activities to trying to deal with the problem of the unmarried Irish mother. We have not mentioned the matter in print or publicly because we know that, large as the problem may be for us, the debt which is owed to the Irish Church by the Catholics of this country can never be measured; and many of our most generous subscribers live in Ireland or remember the land of their birth with an affection which is probably without equal amongst peoples who have been forced to migrate in modern times. We have been reluctant to be a party to discussion which we know is extremely painful to Irish people, but now that an Irish Society has felt the necessity of mentioning this matter publicly, we feel that we should also explain the problem and our silence in the past. We still think that the only reason why the matter needs to be discussed is that, as a result of the open discussion, some effective way can be found of preserving the

Faith of unknown numbers of Catholic children. It needs to be said very definitely and openly that we do know now how many Irish Catholic children are lost to the Faith in this country, and have never been heard of by any Catholic Society in England. The present campaign in England by Irish missioners is most welcome and we equally welcome their co-operation in our work.

"Much could be said of the economic forces which make it impossible for Irish people to earn a living at home, and much more of the enticements of high wages, a higher standard of living, etc., which are offered to the young people of Ireland. Every newspaper, Catholic and National, carries advertisements from Hospitals, Contractors, and private employers inviting them to come over, and it is idle to pretend that we have no responsibility towards those who get into difficulties because the change of atmosphere is too much to cope with. It is not fair to represent the situation as an invasion—England does invite and value the Irish worker.

"Not all of the problem, however, arises from this inability to settle down in strange conditions. In terms of the large numbers of young men and women who come over and remain true to their ideals, the number we are concerned with may be small but the burden on the resources of the Crusade of Rescue is often quite impossible to bear.

"We are therefore grateful to the Catholic Protection and Rescue Society of Ireland, whose offices are in South Anne Street, Dublin, for their frank comments. Our two Societies are old friends. We are in daily correspondence, often on the telephone, and the priests attached to the work on both sides of the Irish Sea are in each others' offices or at conference together several times each year.

"The real tragedy is the arrival of numbers of girls already pregnant. We quote: '. . . *Still many children of Irish Catholic mothers are being lost to the Faith. Reports from the English Catholic Rescue Societies indicate that a great many expectant mothers leave this country annually and go to England for their confinement and dispose of their infants there. The situation appears to be particularly bad in the London area and the Crusade of Rescue, whilst doing magnificent work in helping our Irish girls, reports that it cannot cope with the large numbers—estimated to be many hundreds annually.'*

"'*These children are not lost through proselytising agencies. Many of the mothers first seek Catholic aid, but such aid is limited and the demand on it is so great that the promise of help takes a long time to fulfil. On the other hand, the demand by non-Catholic adopters for infants for adoption far exceeds the supply of non-Catholic children available and the result is that Catholic mothers freely give their babies to non-Catholics who offer affection and a good home to the child. The material standards of these non-Catholic English adoptive homes are often attractive to the unmarried mother anxious to dispose of her child quickly.'*

"The Report speaks of the problem of the girl who gets into difficulties at home, and goes on to say: '*In recent years, we have reported this serious loss of our children. We emphasise it again this year because it is growing considerably and we find that responsible people often recommend young unmarried mothers to hasten off to England some months before the expected date of the confinement. This great and growing evil must be faced and if possible a remedy found to meet it.'*

"We did mention, in our comments in recent numbers of *St. Peter's Net*, this terrible temptation mentioned above, which faces a Catholic unmarried mother. There are, it is said, ten non-Catholic adopters waiting and willing to adopt every child available; the exact reverse is true for Catholic children. We have not the places available quickly enough and unmarried mothers do succumb in large numbers to the temptation. If we cannot place their babies as infants, then the children are lost to the Faith. We do our very best with foster-mothers, our monthly bill in that respect is almost £1,000 and we try to place the babies in Nurseries—our own or those such as Nazareth House. Local Authorities speak of £500 per annum as the cost of keeping a baby in a Nursery. With Nuns doing the work and working tremendously hard, we manage for less.

"The desperate thought which haunts us all the time, in this work, is that, as the report says, the children are rarely lost through non-Catholic proselytisers but simply because the girls have such an overwhelming sense of shame that it outweighs all considerations of their duty to preserve the Faith of the child. We are often embarrassed by the loyalty to principle of non-Catholic Social Workers, who, in spite of the endeavours of the unmarried mother, refer her to us and urge her to do her duty. We can often only answer this great high-principled action with delay and inability to offer a solution quickly enough to avoid disaster. It is a constant puzzle to us that not only in Ireland, but elsewhere, and in England, there can be mothers who will turn their daughters away in their shame. The comments of neighbours are evidently more feared than the danger to the souls of their unborn grandchildren."

In that year the Crusade of Rescue had 322 children at Homes at Enfield and Feltham, and 184 children were boarded out at other Catholic Homes. The expenditure of the Crusade is £100,000 per annum. The Salvage Department, 13 Blenheim Crescent, W11, will send a motor-van once a month to collect waste newspapers and unwanted furniture, etc.

In conclusion here are the legitimate and illegitimate birth-rates since 1950 for Scotland, for England and Wales, and for Eire:

ALL BIRTHS PER THOUSAND OF POPULATION

	Eire	*England & Wales*	*Scotland*
1955	21.17	15.0	18.027
1956	20.98	15.6	18.527

ILLEGITIMATE BIRTHS AS PERCENTAGE OF TOTAL BIRTHS

	Eire	*England & Wales*	*Scotland*
1955	1.75	4.7	4.31
1956	1.92	4.8	4.27

In Eire the legitimate birth-rate is higher and the illegitimate birth-rate is lower than in the two other countries. The Irish illegitimacy figures do not include the girls who came to England for their confinement.

There is a dearth of Catholic married couples who wish to adopt an unwanted child. For every Protestant unwanted child there are ten applications, and applicants may wait for two years before a child is available. For every ten unwanted Catholic children there is only one application for a child. Be it remembered that as a rule Catholics have larger families than Protestants. It would be heroic virtue for any mother to adopt an unwanted child when she has three or more of her own. On the other hand there are childless Catholic couples. To these the unwanted child might bring the happiness they have missed. To carry on its work the Westminster Crusade of Rescue has to collect every year the sum of at least one hundred thousand pounds.

CHAPTER VIII

The Fallen Ladies

*" And through the city streets blown withering
She passed."*

FRANCIS THOMPSON

In the second chapter I mentioned that Tyrone Street, the Red Light Quarter of Dublin, had been cleared up by the Legion of Mary. The Legion of Mary is Ireland's greatest contribution since the Middle Ages to the life of the Catholic Church. It is a lay apostolate that undertakes every form of social service. The first *Praesidium* was formed by seventeen working-class girls in a Dublin slum in 1921. The girls elected an elderly seamstress as a chairman. On the table in front of her was a statue of Our Lady, on her right was the parish priest, and on her left Mr. Frank Duff, the Civil Servant who founded the Legion. The girls agreed to work in pairs and each promised to give at least two hours a week of her spare time to the work. The first task to be undertaken was the visiting of the friendless sick in the Dublin Workhouse Infirmary. This was successful. Every friendless woman in the Infirmary now had a friend to whom she could unburden her troubles. Legionaries are forbidden to give money or material aid. A praesidium, consisting of not more than twenty persons, meets once a week to hear reports and to arrange future work. Later men were admitted to the Legion. Some *praesidia* are for women only, others for men only, and some are mixed. The Legion has never looked back. It is now in every continent, and the Pope has expressed his wish that one or more *praesidia* should be formed in every parish throughout the world.

In 1926 two girls volunteered to visit the brothels in Tyrone Street. They were well received, and in three weeks all the owners of these houses, with five exceptions, agreed to abandon their trade. The five who refused were in debt. As long as five houses remained open the others could not be expected to remain closed. So the Legion went to the Commissioner of Police, who arranged that the whole street would be raided. This was done, and from five houses the prostitutes, bullies, and owners were taken to the police station. After a few hours the prostitutes were released. They were told that this was at the request of the Legion of Mary. Next day the bullies were released. The owners were brought before the Justice and sent to prison. The Legion now learnt that there was considerable ill-feeling against them in Tyrone Street. Whereupon the twenty girls of that Praesidium agreed to brave the opposition and to march through Tyrone Street in procession. This they did. Nothing happened until a girl of eighteen rushed from one of the houses, fell on her knees in front of the procession and cursed them for sending her mother to prison. She was a straight girl although brought up in a brothel. The procession halted. At the top of her voice the girl cursed the Legion. Then some of the onlookers got tired of her tirade. They went into the street and took the girl back to her home. The Legion of Mary passed on. There are now no regular brothels in Dublin.

In Dublin there are plenty of prostitutes, but they now live in their own flats. They are not allowed in the better class bars unless accompanied by a man. The Dublin Police Act of 1842 defined the offence of prostitution as follows:

LOITERING FOR THE PURPOSE OF PROSTITUTION OR SOLICITING.

"Every Common Prostitute or Night Walker loitering or being in any thoroughfare or public place for the purpose of

93

prostitution or solicitation to the annoyance of the inhabitants or passers-by."

This has been amended by Section 16 of the Criminal Law Amendment Act of 1935 which reads:

"16—(1) Every common prostitute who is found loitering in any street, thoroughfare, or other place and importuning or soliciting passers-by for purposes of prostitution or being otherwise offensive to passers-by shall be guilty of an offence under this section and shall on summary conviction thereof be liable, in the case of a first such offence, to a fine not exceeding two pounds or, in the case of a second or any subsequent such offence, to imprisonment for any term not exceeding six months.

(2) The Probation of Offenders Act, 1907, shall apply to offences under this section as if the words "or to the prospects of the moral reclamation of the persons charged" were inserted in sub-section (1) of section 1 of the Act immediately before the words "it is inexpedient to inflict any punishment".

Every night ten pairs of girls from the Legion of Mary are in the streets.   They are pretty girls and are often accosted by men.   They are there to make friends with the prostitutes.

There is no White Slave Traffic in Eire.   Nor do I believe that it exists in the United Kingdom.   In Australia in 1939 I got evidence of the White Slave Traffic.

It was a priest at Melbourne who told me the story of Mexican Rose.   Several months later I met the same priest on a tramcar in Sydney and told him that the thing had haunted me.

"And why not?   Do you object to facing the existence of evil?   My own sleep was disturbed for weeks."

"That story should be published."

"By all means publish it, provided you do not refer to me by name.   And yet you're not the only one to whom I told it, and the others if they read it will know its source."

During 1939 on the Imperial Airways Route from Sydney to England the flying-boats stopped for the night at Towns-ville, Darwin, Sourabaya, Penang, Calcutta, Karachi, Basra, Alexandria, and Bracciano. In that year an Australian priest concerned with ecclesiastical affairs is making the journey by air from Sydney to Lake Bracciano, the seaplane port for Rome. He is in his early thirties, of medium height, with black hair, brown eyes, and even features. Both men and women call him good-looking, and a pleasant voice has contributed to his success as a preacher. He is the only passenger until Singapore where a girl comes on board.

A brunette, not very tall, pretty rather than beautiful, with a cream white skin, she dresses well and knows the cosmetic art. Her manners have the assurance and detachment of a self-confident girl, the kind of girl who gets on fairly well with women and is automatically galvanised into sex appeal as soon as a man enters the room. She speaks English with a foreign accent and loses no time in making herself agreeable to the only male passenger, priest though he be. Yet for all her twenty years she is by no means as sophisticated as she would like to be rated, and claps her hands with childish delight when the plane is approaching Penang, Bangkok, Rangoon, and Akyab, or is passing over interesting places. From a thin chain around her neck there hangs a small silver crucifix.

To the priest her chatter, vivacity, and unfeigned happiness are a welcome interlude in the affairs he has on hand—until she opens her handbag. The contents are startling, and with some knowledge of precious stones he appraises the jewellery in that handbag to be worth at least one thousand pounds.

"Surely it's rather unwise to carry so much jewellery in your handbag?"

"Now don't you worry, Father. It's safe enough on the plane."

"But when you're off the plane?"

"Don't you worry. We Mexican girls are sure able to look after ourselves. Hard boiled, I'd say. I'm no dumb doll, and I know my way all around and about. Why, I've been two and a half years in the Marcus Show, the greatest Leg Show ever seen on Broadway. That's what the New York papers said, but make no mistake, Father, it was clean. Not a spot of dirt from hors-d'œuvres to dessert."

"So I've been told."

"Sure you'd be told. We toured the States, New Zealand, and Australia. There was a garden scene where I sang a song called Mexicali Rose, and they used to call me 'Mexican Rose' —wasn't that just too sweet of them? I'd say it was; because our Mexican rose—not me but the flower—is really lovely. We shed a few of our girls on the way: three in the States and two in Australia. Married rich guys. Had to be rich to buy them out of the show. There's quite a big penalty clause for breaking a three years' contract. Guess I wouldn't marry abroad. No, sir, I'm going to marry my fiancé in Mexico City, and I'll soon be home. Mexico City! Mexico City! and she claps her hands.

"Well, you'll be home sooner than if you'd gone via Hong Kong."

"You bet I will, and in India I'll be staying for a few days in a Rajah's palace."

"A Rajah!"

"Sure thing. Didn't you hear about it? A Rajah bought me out of the show and gave me all these presents. Say— Father—I know just what you're thinking now—and you're dead wrong. I'm on the level. Don't you believe me?"

"Yes, I believe you. How did this happen?"

"At Singapore, guess I felt homesick after two and a half years away. This Rajah took me out to dinner, and I just told him all about it. He's on the level or I'm a dumb doll. Likes to be kind, and he's rich I'd say. He's sure kind, and all these presents are not for me. The diamond headdress is for

Mother, and the bracelets are for my sisters. The gold cigarette-case with the ruby inlay is for my fiancé. What do you think of that? Only the necklace is mine. Now do you understand, Father?"

"Perfectly. Go ahead."

"Not much more. He's paying my fare home. Look—here's my ticket on this plane as far as India, and here's my first-class reservations on the *Rex* from Naples to New York, on the *Oriente* from New York to Vera Cruz, and on the train from Vera Cruz to Mexico City. In India I'll stop a few days at his palace, and then he'll take me to see the Taj Mahal, and then to Calcutta where I'll get another plane to Bracciano. The ticket for that bit of the journey is waiting me at Calcutta—and with the agents for Imperial Airways. You see, the Rajah had to hurry back to India, and I couldn't go with him because the Marcus management were hostile. He told me not to worry, and sent me to stay with a lady. Look—here's her card. Gee, she had some fine house. She soon fixed things up with the Marcus people, and I'd say she's clever. Speaks English, French, German, Italian and Spanish. I'd say she's clever."

"Yes, clever as the Devil, and now I'm off to do some work."

In his cabin the priest took out a small note-book in which he wrote the name and address of a woman—for the information of the British authorities at Singapore. This done he lit a cigarette and began to think of the problem in hand. The girl was in danger and it was his duty to try to save her, possibly from herself—most difficult of all salvage.

He could tell her the truth about India—that everything in Katherine Mayo's *Mother India* was true, but was only a fraction of the truth; that the Government Commission's Report on Child Marriage had never been published and could never be published without shocking the conscience of the civilised world: that outside British India, there was a White Slave

Traffic both in women and European boys; that what she as a Catholic knew to be mortal sins were as nothing compared with the vices of India; and that outside British India orgies were staged to which the word bestial could not be applied without insulting the brute creation. If he told her of these things, she would not believe him.

From her nationality and the little silver crucifix he knew that she had been baptised in the Faith. Yet to take that line might arouse her obstinacy.

The girl liked him and he could cultivate her friendship. Yet a priest must be circumspect and avoid occasions of scandal, for he is watched by eyes not always friendly. From a chance remark by one of the crew he knew that the story of the Rajah was known on board. If he spent too much time with the girl, they might think he was trying to take the Rajah's place.

His only hope was to take every opportunity to sow the seeds of distrust in her mind, and this would have to be done in less than forty-two hours.

"How do you know your friend is a Rajah?"

"He told me, and I'd say he's very rich."

"Quite likely, but many Indians are very rich without being Rajahs."

"Do you think your fiancé would like the idea of your staying in a Rajah's palace?"

"He just wouldn't understand. He'd be jealous. But wait till he sees the cigarette-case."

"If you were an Australian girl, and they're independent enough, you wouldn't be allowed to visit this Rajah."

"Who'd stop me?"

"The Australian Government. A few years back a number of good-looking Australian girls were offered highly paid posts, too highly paid posts, as secretaries or typists to some of these so-called Rajahs. Those who went—just disappeared."

"India's a huge country, and only a part is under British rule. You're not a British subject, and I don't know of any Mexican Consuls. You don't know any of the two hundred Indian languages, and if anything went wrong there'd be no one to help you. Now I happen to know the Italian Consul at Calcutta, and if you give me your name and home address I'll get him to give you a *Salve Conductore*. That will put you under the protection of the Italian Government as long as you're in India. At least someone will be interested in what happens to you. In India that Mexican passport of yours is just about as much use as a sick headache. I'm going to see the Consul in any case tomorrow evening at seven, and the plane arrives at five past six. I could fix up your Salve Conductore at the same time. Won't you let me do that for you?"

"Thank you, Father, I'll—think it over."

"Say, Father, you're real kind. I figure I'd better have that *Salve Conductore*. Not that I'm likely to need it."

"I'll see to it."

The captain of the flying-boat and the priest are standing on the Imperial Airways jetty at Calcutta. Ahead of them the girl, carrying her handbag, is walking towards the barrier, and the captain smiles.

"Now you'll see some fireworks. If she thinks she'll be allowed to land here with that passport of hers—she's very much mistaken."

To their astonishment the girl, without the slightest difficulty passes through the barrier and into the roadway.

"Hell," says the captain, "these Babus have been bribed. Let's hurry, and see where she's going."

At the barrier they see the girl being driven away in a limousine, with two Sikhs in front.

"Hell!"

"It may still be all right, captain. Perhaps he's booked her accommodation for the night in one of the hotels."

"I hope he has. She told me all about your *Salve Conductore*, but I've a better plan. I'm wiring the authorities to stop her from landing, and whether she likes it or not, I'm taking her on to Italy at the Company's expense."

Half an hour later a Sikh comes down to the jetty to see the captain and salaams: "Your lady passenger will not proceed with you tomorrow."

"Oh yes, by God she will. This plane does not leave without her." Yet he knows the bluff is in vain.

Again the Sikh salaams. "The message is—your lady passenger will not proceed with you tomorrow."

At seven o'clock in the Italian Consulate the priest tells his story and the Consul comments: "In the ordinary way all foreigners landing in India are seen by the police and sign a declaration which includes the address to which they are proceeding. Any change of address must be notified. For the first twelve months they are watched, although they are unaware of the fact, by the C.I.D. who are most efficient. On the other hand, I don't suppose much attention is paid to those rich birds of passage who travel by air and come ashore to spend the night in an hotel. No doubt the Babus were bribed to let her pass, and a hundred rupees will go a long way in that direction. There's no clue to the man's identity, and the passages to Mexico City would be booked through intermediaries.

"The plane ticket was most likely intended to mislead anyone who tried to find her. He certainly would have nothing to do with the Rajah's Palace he told her about, and probably came from a different part of India. He'll get back all his presents. Most of the passage money will be refunded if the tickets are cancelled in time. That girl will never leave India. I give her six months in his harem, and then she'll be sent to the Bazaar. Within a year, if she's lucky enough to lay her hands on a razor, she'll cut her throat."

Five days later in Rome, a haunted priest enters the offices of the Italian line. He is there to inquire about a passage that was booked in the *Rex*. Passage had been cancelled by cable.

That is a sad story, one of the saddest I know. Yet the review of that story by one of my critics in Eire throws a strange light on his mentality.

Mr. John Crawford in a two-column review of this book in the *Irish Press* of 29th September 1956, wrote, "He thinks about the White Slave Traffic, and there follows a long and totally irrelevant story about India, which had whiskers on it when Katherine Mayo wrote her masterpiece of misrepresentation, *Mother India*.

The story of Mexican Rose was told to me by an Australian priest. I have no reason to think he was not telling me the truth. In 1939, I was in India for three weeks. I asked Dr. Roberts, the Catholic Archbishop of Bombay, if Katherine Mayo's book *Mother India* was true; he replied—"Yes, it's true, but it's only one-tenth of the truth. The Government dare not publish the Report of the Commission on child marriages. It would have shocked the conscience of the civilised world." It is probable that the Catholic Archbishop of Bombay knew more about India than my reviewer.

The title of this chapter is from the poem by Francis Thompson to the young girl Ann who found him destitute in London.

> And of her own scant pittance did she give
> that I might eat and live.

"The generous girl, without a murmur, paid out of her own humble purse, at a time, be it remembered, when she had scarcely wherewithal to purchase the bare necessities of life, and when she could have no reason to expect that I should ever be able to reimburse her.

"O youthful benefactress! how often in succeeding years, standing in solitary places, and thinking of thee with grief of heart and perfect love—how often have I wished that, as in ancient times the curse of a father was believed to have a supernatural power, and to pursue its object with a fatal necessity of fulfilment, even so the benediction of a heart appraised with gratitude might have a like prerogative, might have power given it from above to chase, to haunt, to waylay, to pursue thee into the central darkness of a London brothel, or (if it were possible) even into darkness of the grave, there to awaken thee with an authentic message of peace and forgive ness, and of final reconciliation."[1]

But what of the character of these girls? A woman probation officer tells me that whereas female thieves boast of chastity, prostitutes boast of being honest. And most of them are honest. Some are not too intelligent and all are lazy or work-shy. Yet those who know them best say that many have the Christian virtues of humility and of charity.

A policeman whose beat is in Hyde Park, London, served a girl with a summons to appear before the magistrate on the following day for a breach of the police regulations. She had been found alone in a shrubbery which by Regulation 62 is out of bounds to the public. For breach of Regulation 62 you may be fined up to five pounds. On receiving the summons she asked—"Can this be taken in the morning?"

"Why?" said the policeman.

"One of the girls is dead. She died in hospital. She died of cancer and had no relatives and no money. So some of us have subscribed for her funeral. It's tomorrow afternoon and I want to be there."

Next morning at Bow Street Police Station the girl was fined ten shillings. In the afternoon she went to the funeral.

Francis Thompson had sought in vain for the girl who had given him food and shelter when she found him destitute on the Embankment. So he wrote a poem in her honour. I never thanked the lady who helped me in one of my darkest hours, but this is the story.

On a bright May morning I was working with my secretary

[1] *Francis Thompson and Wilfrid Meynell.* A Memoir by Viola Meynell. Hollis & Carter Ltd., London 1952.

in the library whose windows overlook the terrace. Along the terrace came a chauffeur-driven limousine which stopped at our gate. The chauffeur got out, came up the steps, rang the bell, delivered a message, and then drove away.

"That's curious," said my secretary.

A moment later the maid handed me a letter. "He said there was no reply."

I opened the letter. It was from the private secretary of one of my patients who, so the letter said, had decided with great reluctance and regret to accept the advice of his counsellors and dispense with my services as his doctor. He would continue to take the same interest in me and my affairs as in the past. Would I please sent my account.

I handed the letter to my secretary who having read it said: "Even a servant is entitled to notice, but they dismiss you like this. Once I thought I might be interested in your religion, but never again." She dried her eyes and continued typing.

Never before had I seen her in tears, and I did not point out the flaw in her reasoning. I could have quoted Hilaire Belloc who said that if anyone had told Alexander I there was too much poisoning in Vatican circles, the Pope could have replied that poisoning did not affect the power of the Keys. That is true and to say the contrary is heresy. So I left the house and went for a long walk.

I walked to the top of the Tottenham Court Road where I saw a small public-house which I had not previously visited. I entered the four-ale bar. It was almost deserted but round the walls were wooden rectangular tables with wooden benches. I bought a drink and sat down. At the next table was a fat, flouncing blowzy woman with peroxide hair and aged between 40 and 50. She smiled ingratiatingly. I scowled at her and bought myself another drink.

On returning to the table I noticed that the woman had been joined by another somewhat younger woman. I overheard their conversation. They were on the way to a V.D.

Clinic where they were to receive an intravenous injection for syphilis. They were discussing the effect on the injections of the gin they were now drinking. The doctor had told them not to drink. Disgusting. I went for another drink, and as I ordered my third whisky the barman looked at me curiously. I cursed myself for having a speaking face. Then I returned to my table and determined to curse the world in general.

I cursed the man who had been an *agent provocateur,* for in my opinion the *agent provocateur,* whoever he be, is among the most degraded of mankind. I cursed myself for having walked into a blatant trap. I cursed the Sunday newspaper that published a spurious interview in which I commented on the health of my patient. There had been no interview. The whole thing was an invention. I cursed myself for having told a man that I contemplated legal proceedings. These would have been abhorrent to my patient. Strange to say I did not curse the patient whom I knew to be a very sick man.

The two women rose to go and as they passed my table the older one bent towards me and spoke the words that follow—"Laddie, I don't know what your trouble is, but remember there's a day called Tomorrow." Before I could answer, she was in the street.

She was right. The past had been my fault and there was a day called Tomorrow. I left the pub, got on a bus home, and told my wife of this strange adventure. I had never thanked the lady in the pub, but I believe that for her kindness to me she will receive on the Great Day of Judgment high commendation.

CHAPTER IX

The Cursing Stones

AFTER breakfast one morning in the Galway County Club I was talking to Mr. Eoin O'Mahony, a short stout middle-aged bearded barrister from Dublin, a most agreeable companion. He gave me eighteen introductions to his friends in Eire and wrote eighteen letters to endorse these introductions. He has an accurate knowledge of the family history of every noted family in Ireland. While we were talking Father Quinn called and introduced himself as our parish priest. His church, St. Patrick's, was on the eastern side of the square. He had his car and offered to run us round the city of Galway. We accepted with pleasure. The city of Galway, on the eastern bank of the Corrib River at the north end of Galway Bay, is said to be the ancient Mangata described by Ptolemy. In the reign of Henry III of England in 1232 it was captured by a force of Anglo-Normans under Richard de Burgo. They fortified the city against the surrounding Irish and made it a great centre of trade. Many Irish families are descended from these Anglo-Normans. Their families include the Blakes, Bodkins, Brownes, D'Arcys, ffrenches, Kiernans, Sherrets and Morrisses. In 1651 the city surrendered to Cromwell's troops under Sir Charles Coote. The Anglo-Norman families were called by Cromwell the "Galway Tribes". In 1691 the city surrendered to the troops of William of Orange.

Off the main street are the ruins of the Lion's Tower. The height of its massive masonry indicates the strength of the Norman fortifications. Father Quinn regretted that the City

Council had not adopted his idea of putting a statue of Our Lady in the ruins. In the main street is St. Nicholas Church, built by the Normans in 1320. In this church Columbus is said to have heard Mass before sailing in the *Santa Maria* to discover the New World. It is certain that his crew included one man Rice de Culvey who came from the city of Galway. Some say it was a brother of Columbus who heard Mass in St. Nicholas. In that case he probably took Rice de Culvey back to Spain to support the projected voyage across the Western Ocean. These Galway sailors had been far into the Atlantic. The Vikings appear to have been the first to reach America, because one of their watch towers has been found on Rhode Island.

Near St. Nicholas is the ruined wall of the old prison. On the wall is a skull and crossbones in black marble and this inscription: "This memorial of the stern and unbending justice of the chief magistrate of this City, James Lynch Fitzstephen elected mayor, A.D. 1493, who condemned and executed his own guilty son, Walter, on this spot."

The story is that a young Spaniard was staying at the Mayor's house as his guest. The Mayor's son and the Spaniard fought over a girl and the Spaniard was killed. The public executioner refused to hang the Mayor's son, so that the Mayor hanged his own son from the window you now see.

Near the shore is the Spanish Arch. Through this gate the Spanish sailors and merchants entered the city. In those days there were no docks, and ships were moored at the mouth of the Corrib River a little way to the west. Galway had a great trade with Spain and imported wines and hides in exchange for wool. Yet I do not think there is any evidence either from names or from architecture that the Spanish merchants ever settled in Galway. In the main street a narrow covered passage, called in Scotland a close, led to a courtyard behind two old buildings. On each side of the courtyard a stone staircase mounted to the first floor of the building. I have seen a similar arrangement in Old Edinburgh. By closing the passage the occupants of the houses could protect themselves against unwelcome visitors. Father Quinn called the courtyard a "patio". It was unlike any "patio" that ever I saw in Spain.

The modern city of Galway has a large number of butchers' shops and public-houses. In no other city have I ever seen so many. Every sixth shop seemed to be one or the other. The barrister Mr. Eoin O'Mahony told me that when a publican gave up his licence the other publicans had to pay him compensation. This caused some ill-feeling. If a beershop at the docks closed, its customers were not likely to go to the bar at the Great Western Hotel. Yet the hotel had to pay compensation.

In Ireland in the sixteenth century were many friends of Spain and one of the old songs contains these lines:

> The Spanish ships are on the way,
> My dark Rosaleen . . .

This makes the more strange the fate of those Spaniards who escaped from the three ships of the Armada that were wrecked on the west coast of Ireland between Donegal and Clare. The survivors on reaching the shore were murdered by the native Irish. This was the land that Philip II had planned to liberate from the yoke of England. The truth is that Ireland, then as now, was divided. Many of the Irish Chieftains, such as "the Queen's O'Connor" supported the English ascendency, and the Spanish ships had the misfortune to be wrecked on hostile parts of the coast. At least one Spaniard escaped. He was a Grandee, but the Irish robbed him of his clothes, and he spent the winter dressed in straw. He spoke Latin and finally contacted a Bishop who put him on a ship for the Low Countries where the Spanish Government paid five pounds for every repatriated sailor from the Armada.

On April 20th I had lunch with Professor Conor O'Malley,

the ophthalmologist. At lunch there was his wife, who is consultant at the Galway Hospital, his son, and a daughter. I mention the date because the weather was so mild that we lunched on the lawn in the shade of a sycamore tree. Afterwards Professor Conor O'Malley motored me round Lough Corrib. The Lough is 27 miles long and lies north of the city of Galway. From the Lough the Corrib River, three miles long, runs to Galway Bay which it enters west of the city. In the spring the river below the weir is blocked with salmon to whom this short river gives access to 50,000 acres of lake water. On the western side of the Lough were several small villages in which were a large number of grocers' shops. Each shop was owned by a man who had come from the surrounding countryside, and his previous neighbours remained his customers. Not a large turnover. At the north-western end of the Lough we turned east and passed a hill on which the heather was on fire. The road acted as a brake and the wind was not strong enough to blow the fire across. The road then went southwards through a narrow valley between hills of sheep with here and there a shepherd's house. In addition to his salary a shepherd has his house, some acres of ground on which he can keep a cow, and is entitled to run a score of his own sheep. Some shepherds are said to be wealthier than their masters. Unless the master can walk the hills and see what is happening, the shepherd may own most of the sheep!

At the small village of Kilmilkin we went into the church, where I saw the last stained-glass window to be made by the late Miss Evie Hone, the Dublin artist. The window is based on the tradition that the O'Malley Clan, called in the annals men of Umhall, were slaughtered by the Danes in a raid in 889. Only one sickly male child of the chieftain line was left. A seer told the mother to take the child to Inis Gloira, an island off the coast of Mayo sacred to St. Brendan the Navigator, and dip him in the blessed well there. Whereon he was restored to health by the power of St. Brendan and became the warrior leader of the clan. The window depicts the mother and child at the well with St. Brendan dominating the scene. In the background is the sea with the Saint's ship; a monulan and a beehive clahan. A stone with the O'Malley arms and the inscription in Irish says the window is erected to the memory of John Francis O'Malley, M.Ch., F.R.C.S., a well-known surgeon of Harley Street.

At the south-eastern end of the Lough we went into a country hotel *de luxe* for a drink. On the cocktail bar in a glass dish were small cold cooked portions of bacon rind. As an appetiser for a drink I prefer olives or anchovies. I asked the barman what the hotel charged per week.

"Four pounds."

The place looked more like four pounds per day. The barman was a foreigner and had probably misunderstood my question. So I asked him: "Are you a Pole?"

"No, I am French."

"*Bon. Combien est la pension dans cet hotel pour la semaine?*"

"You speak bad French."

I abandoned the unequal contest. Then Professor O'Malley told me that once when a boy he had gone with his father to an Italian restaurant in London. His father had tried his Italian on the waiter. The man who had not understood a word then said: "Signore, from what part of Italy do you come?"

That was tact.

Another day I took the bus to Clifden, a sleepy country town three miles from the Atlantic at the far end of Connemara. The road led through a beautiful land of moors, lakes, and rivers. There were few houses. Far in the west are the twelve Bens. These twelve cone-shaped mountains rise straight from the moorland. In the bus were three Scotswomen. They were school-teachers from Perth, and on the way the bus conductor gave them much of the history of Ireland. On the return journey one of the teachers said to me: "I wonder how many bus conductors in Scotland know the history of Wallace and the War of Independence."

Very different is the scenery in the east of Connaught. Once I stayed at Castle Donamon near the county town of Roscommon. This twelfth-century castle is now occupied by the Society of the Divine Word. In front is the river Suck, and standing on the bridge I could not tell which way the water was flowing. The speed of this tributary of the Shannon is probably measured in inches per hour. From the top of the castle one saw all round a plain of bog-land over which the clouds hung low. This dismal scene gave point to Cromwell's boast that he would drive the Irish "to Hell or to Connaught".

Professor Conor O'Malley told me that 160 years ago an attempt had been made to use the Cursing Stones against his grandfather, who was a large grazier. A Mr. X had asked the blacksmith to use the stones. The blacksmith lived at Maumeen-a-gowan (Pass of the blacksmith) in the Maum Valley. He refused. Some days later Mr. X called at the smithy and gave the blacksmith a drink of poisoned poteen. The blacksmith died. There was an inquest but no post-mortem. The verdict was death from natural causes, but the people believed he had been poisoned.

To make Cursing Stones you place twelve stones in a circle like the hours of a clock. Working anti-clockwise you then turn each stone, and as you turn it you say the Lord's Prayer backwards and ask the Devil to curse your enemy. In the Irish language this practice is called "Turning the flagstones". That is a euphemism for this nefarious piece of Black Magic.

From Galway I went north to Sligo. Here, the Spanish Ambassador's son had advised me, I would hear more about the "Cursing Stones". It was a five-and-a-half-hour journey by bus through open dairy country. At Sligo I stayed at the Grand Hotel, 15s 6d. bed and breakfast; from my barrister friend in Galway I had an introduction to the senior surgeon of the Sligo Hospital. He was away in Dublin but within half an hour his wife had put me in touch with two local antiquarians; one was Mr. Patrick Tohall (pronounced Toll) C.B.E. He was a retired civil engineer from the Irish Land Commission and knew the history of Land in Ireland from the time of the Norman Conquest. In the eighteenth century landlords in the West, mostly English and absentees, raised rents to 10 per cent above the value of farm produce. If the farm produce was worth ten pounds, rent was eleven pounds. This was intended to force the farmers to take up weaving. By this they could make a living and pay for the privilege of working the farm for the benefit of the landlord. This led to the Land War of 1789 and the shooting of landlords or their agents. In the confessional a priest said to the farmer who had said he had shot his landlord: "Confess your sins, you are not here to talk politics." On another occasion the farmers were waiting, one on either side of the hedge by the roadside, to shoot the landlord, who always drove past that way at 5 p.m. By six o'clock he had not appeared. "He's late," called one farmer from behind the hedge. "Indeed, and he is," said the other, "I hope nothing has happened to the poor man."

Mr. Tohall told me that the Cursing Stones had been used against an English warship. This was the *Wasp* sunk by running on the rocks off Tory Island, Co. Donegal, on 22nd September, 1884. The ship had been sent to overawe the islanders into paying rates. They turned the *Clocha Breaca* ("Speckled Stones")—probably "pocked" stones as the antiquarians say—against the ship, and sure enough she was wrecked and lay there derelict for fifty years. Mr. Tohall also told me that the "water-horse" was not a mythical animal but a real killer. It was the seventh son of an otter and weighed 40 lb. The water-horse was also known in the Western Isles of Scotland and at the north end of Barra I had seen the loch of the water-horse. In the *Journal of The Royal Society of Antiquaries of Ireland* (Vol. LXXVIII 1948) Mr. Tohall gives a photograph of the effigy of a "water-horse" on a tombstone in the cemetery of Congbhail. This tombstone commemorates Grainne, the wife of a man McLoughlin. "She took some clothes down to the lakeshore to wash them. As she did not return her husband went to look for her and found her bloody body by the lake-side with the Dobhar-chú asleep on her breast. Returning to the house for his dagger he stole silently on the Dobhar-chú and drove the knife into its breast. Before it died, however, it whistled to call its fellow; and the old people of the place, who knew the ways of the animals, warned McLoughlin to fly for his life. He took to horse, another mounted man accompanying him. The second Dobhar-chú came swimming from the lake and pursued the pair. Realising that they could not shake it off they stopped near some old walls and drew their horses across an open door. The Dobhar-chú rushed under the horses' legs to attack the men, but as it emerged from beneath them one of the men stabbed and killed it."

From Dr. Hegarthy of Sligo I got information about the "Cursing Stones" on the island of Inishmurray. The island had belonged to his grandfather until he was compelled to exchange it for land on the mainland. His mother had been the school-teacher on the island. She had a class of twenty-five children and the number never dropped below ten. Had it done so she would have been regarded as a part-time teacher. The island is five-and-a-half miles west of Streedagh Point and fourteen miles north of Sligo. St. Molaise founded his monastery on Inishmurray in 530. Here he gave the penance to Colmcille, afterwards known as Saint Columba, "that he must leave Ireland and never return until he had won for Christ as many souls as he had caused to die in battle". In the monastery grounds a stone is inscribed to Colmcille. The monastery grounds in the form of an ellipse cover an area of three-quarters of an acre. They are now surrounded by a massive wall from eight to twenty feet high and ten feet wide. It is believed the wall was not built until the Vikings began raiding the west coast of Ireland. In the wall there were cells for the monks. The wall itself follows an irregular pattern and goes out of its way to include some stone buildings within the monastery grounds. One of these has a beehive roof—a roof made of flat stones, each stone overlapping the stone on which it rests. One archaeologist pronounced the building to be identical with the Charnel Houses of Greece. Local archaeologists now accept the view that the island was once a pre-Christian Druid settlement. The Druids built sixteen tables, each consisting of a flat stone three feet square, resting on other stones about three feet above the ground. Eleven of these tables are around the coast of the island and the remaining five are now within the walls of the monastery. It is said the monks converted these tables into Stations of the Cross— sixteen instead of the usual Catholic fourteen. This must have been done after the twelfth century because in that century the Franciscans who were in charge of the Holy Places in Jerusalem began the devotion of the Stations of the Cross.

To make the Stations at Inishmurray the monks walked along the south coast and then back to the monastery by the north coast, a distance of about four miles. The monastery is at the eastern end of the island, near the place where a small boat may land if the Atlantic swell be not too heavy.

The twelfth Station of the Cross or the first within the walls of the monastery contains the Cursing Stones. This table differs from the others in having two flat vertical stones, one resting on either edge of the table. On the table itself are the Cursing Stones, fifty-one in number. These are loose stones which vary from the size of your fist to that of a football. It is said to be impossible to count them and get the right number at the end of each count. About one-third of the stones are engraved with a Cross. One stone is oblong, 14 inches high, 5 inches wide, and 4 inches deep. This has been hollowed to form a bottle. Another stone is mushroom-shaped and the stalk of the mushroom fits into the neck of the bottle and acts as a stopper. This stone is supposed to have contained the Chrysm.

To use the Cursing Stones you must make the Stations of the Cross in reverse order. You begin in the monastery grounds at the sixteenth table and on coming to the twelfth you turn each of the fifty-one stones. At the turning of each stone you curse your enemy. Then you walk four miles round the island and make the other Stations of the Cross. After all that something ought to happen—either to your enemy or to yourself. I am sorry I cannot tell you what the two extra Stations were. I am neither a theologian nor an archaeologist, nor even an antiquary. So do not write to me. Yet when a boy I showed some promise as an antiquarian by being able to translate the inscription said to have been inscribed on a large earthenware bowl that was found near the Roman Wall between Forth and Clyde. It read: *iti sapis potandis abigone*.

There are no Cursing Stones in Scotland: this would appear an Irish privilege.

In recent times the population of Inishmurray was never more than ten families and these were fewer when the island was abandoned in 1947. The families were given Council homes with half an acre of land on the mainland at Streeagh Point. By fishing, by working as general labourers, and by cultivating their half-acre of land they could then earn a living. They had left Inishmurray owing to the failure of their main industry—the making of poteen. Originally this was made from home-grown barley but frequent visits from the Royal Irish Constabulary made it difficult to conceal the preparation of the barley. So they bought barrels of treacle. This was diluted with water, fermented with yeast, and distilled. They used a water-cooled copper worm and the whole business could be done in five days. The Government became aware of this and stopped the sale of treacle in barrels to unauthorised persons. No one could buy more than 2 lb. of treacle at a time. The islanders then used brown sugar. This took longer to ferment and finally they used white sugar. Then came World War II. Sugar was rationed and the industry destroyed.

Poteen has a curious smell. No doubt if it were matured for seven years like good Scotch whisky it would improve. Being illegal, poteen is always sold as soon as made. The islanders sold their poteen to the mainland. There you could hide your poteen in the bog, but you might be seen by a neighbour who at night would raid your hidden cellar. Poteen drinkers drink the stuff neat and then take a glass of water. They are drinking crude alcohol but it is not wood alcohol and Professor Conor O'Malley, the ophthalmologist tells me he has never seen a case of blindness caused by poteen.

Poteen is not to be had in Great Britain, but I advise readers to have a care about the national beverage of Scotland, of which the best blends are now exported. By our national beverage I mean the real Mackay, well blended and mature. Beware fancy names such as Sutherland's Highland Storm. The label depicts a distillery struck by lightning and conceals a bottled headache. Above all, as you value your life, shun the awful fire-water that is crude white spirit coloured with cold tea. It is made and bottled in Lower Pimlico. In its wake are evil things—heartaches, madness, death, and damnation.

CHAPTER X

On the Road to Doneraile

FROM Sligo I went by bus north to Donegal. I wanted to see more of the west coast. This coast is mostly flat except at the north-west and south-west. The road went inland and did not reach the sea until south of Donegal. Here we passed the village of Bundoran whose esplanade overlooks the Atlantic. Every house and shop was newly painted in bright blues and greens. This was in readiness for the summer visitors who come from the Republic and from Northern Ireland.

At Donegal the bus stopped at the base of a green in the centre of the town. The green is an isosceles triangle which for some reason unknown to me is called the Diamond. At the bus stop was the Abbey Hotel into which I went. This is a small commercial hotel, clean with good cooking. Terms 12s. 6d. bed and breakfast. Here I met a commercial traveller from Dublin. His firm made men's ready-made clothing and he said this was his best time just before the summer holidays. I asked him if there were any Jews in his firm. "Yes, we have one Jew and we couldn't do without him. We had an Irishman in charge of our workshop. He had been trained in England, but the other workers thought he was just one of themselves and would not obey him. So we put a Jew in charge." He also said that in Dublin people prefer to work for a Protestant rather than a Catholic employer.

The summer buses to the north of Donegal Bay and to the mountains beyond were not yet running. So after looking at the river Eske and at the ruins of an ancient castle and a still more ancient monastery, fully described in the guide-book,

I returned to the city of Galway. From Galway I went by bus
to Limerick. The road goes through County Clare which has
more lakes than any other county in Ireland. From the bus
I saw many lakes. Some of them are little larger than large
ponds, which shows how waterlogged is Eire. Once in
London I had met an Irishman who was on holiday. He was
a water diviner and with his partner ran a successful business in
Eire. He ended by saying: "When a client cannot afford our
fee for visiting his property I tell him to bring to our office a
large map of the district. This I place on the floor. Then I
walk over it and the divining rod works as well as if I was
walking over the ground."

"Yes," I said, "except on the top of a mountain it's quite
safe to detect water anywhere in Eire."

Limerick is a beautiful city near the mouth of the Shannon.
Its charter is older than that of London. I stayed one night
at the Glentworth Hotel. Bed and breakfast, 19s. 6d. After
dinner Mr. Thomas O'Donnell called to see me. He had the
address from Mr. Eoin O'Mahony. We talked about the causes
of late marriages in Eire. Mr. O'Donnell is a solicitor, and
he thought the main cause was that the eldest son does not
come into possession of the farm until his father's death.
An Irishman did not like to make his will. Ninety per cent
of the wills he had drawn up were made by a man on his sick-
bed. A farmer would be brought into Limerick Hospital late
at night for an immediate operation. The doctor would ask:
"Are your affairs in order?" The answer was usually:
"No." So a solicitor was summoned and the will was made.
He said that every solicitor in Eire would bear this out. Many
of the farmhouses were also old-fashioned. A girl from the
city would refuse to make her home in a house that lacked
indoor sanitation.

Our conversation was interrupted at 10 p.m. when a bell-
boy told me I was wanted on the telephone.

"This is the Tourist Association of Killarney. We had

your address from Mr. Eoin O'Mahony, and wondered when you are coming to Killarney?"

"But I'm not going to Killarney. I'm on my way to Doneraile."

"You're not coming to Killarney? One moment please— (a long pause). The Tourish Association will be glad if you will come as our guest for two days."

"Can you send a car?"

"To Limerick?"

"Yes."

"That's a long way. You could get a bus in the morning to Tralee. We could meet you there with a car at twelve noon."

"Then how shall I get to Doneraile?"

"From Killarney you can get a train to Mallow, the nearest town to Doneraile."

"Many thanks. I shall be at Tralee by noon tomorrow."

I rejoined Mr. O'Donnell and told him I must decline his kind offer to show me round Limerick in the morning. And so to bed, where I heard the Atlantic planes as they roared overhead to Shannon Airport fifteen miles to the east of Limerick.

By noon next day I was at Tralee where Mr. Donal O'Cahill met me with a car from Killarney. On the way I said to him: "In Eire I don't know what to believe. What a man says to me one day may be contradicted by another man the next day."

"Yes, what a man says one day is contradicted by another man the next day, but what 'The Man' tells you will never be contradicted."

From that cryptic remark I surmised he had belonged to the Irish Republican Army. Soon he told me of his experiences as a hunger-striker. "In Ireland the hunger-strike made fools of the English. After forty-eight hours they let us out of prison. Then I and others found ourselves in prison in Belfast. There they did not release us, and we knew the English Government meant business when they moved us to London.

We crossed in a destroyer and the sea was rough. Those who were seasick had a terrible time. They retched but had nothing to bring up except blood. It was terrible to see them. When we got to London we were sent to Wormwood Scrubbs Prison. I became delirious, but every night I could hear the Irish saying the Rosary outside the prison."

The Lord Mayor of Cork, Terence MacSwiney, died in Brixton Prison after seventy-three days of self-enforced starvation. A man may starve himself to death but he cannot thirst himself to death, and I suspect that the prison authorities had added white of egg to the water that he drank. At all events, his death shocked the conscience of the English. Bishop Amigo of Southwark sang a Solemn Requiem High Mass, and thousands of Irish followed the coffin to Euston Station. Later hunger-strikers were released and sent to London hospitals for treatment.

The Lake of Killarney is in three parts. The largest and most northerly is called the Lower Lake. It is also called Lough Lene and Lake Lein. All three names appear in the guide-book. From this lake the river Laune runs to the sea at Castlemaine Bay. Every year 20,000 salmon are taken from the river. The lake is five-and-a-half miles long and three miles broad. It has thirty islands. To the south-east and separated by a peninsula is Muckross Lake. This is also called Torc Lake. It is two miles long and a mile broad. To the south is the smallest lake. It is called the Upper Lake, and is two miles long and half a mile wide, From this lake a river called the Long Range runs north-east to Lake Muckross. Near Lake Muckross the river divides and sends a branch into the Lower Lake. The place where the river divides into two is called "The Meeting of the Waters!" This is the place "where Sir Walter Scott, roused from reverie, exclaimed: 'Ah, this is beautiful!'"[1].

[1] Quoted in *Killarney: Land and Lake,* by Donal O'Cahill. The Cliona Press, Dublin. 8th edition, p. 36.

I am sorry for any child who has to learn the geography of Killarney.

The town of Killarney where I stayed for two nights at the International Hotel is about two miles to the east of the north shore of the Lower Lake. It is a clean pleasant country town, and has a cathedral by Pugin. There is also a beautiful Franciscan church. In the afternoon Mr. O'Cahill and I were driven in a Tourist Association car to Kate Kearney's Cottage. This is to the west of the Lower Lake and at the entrance to the Gap of Dunloe. I do not know who Kate Kearney was but she appears to have been what in Scotland we call 'a bit of a bisum'.

Kate Kearney's Cottage is a repository of picture postcards and souvenirs. At the far end is a bar. Here I was introduced to the proprietor who is said to be a descendent of Kate Kearney. He went to the living-room and returned with a copy of *Arches of the Years* which he asked me to autograph. This I did.

"And what will you drink, doctor?"

"A little poteen, please."

"I'm sorry we have none, but there's plenty of Irish whisky."

"No, thanks."

"Gin?"

"Thank you."

He poured out for us two half-tumblers of neat gin. This I diluted with ginger beer.

We went outside to the waiting car. In the forenoon saddled ponies surround the cottage. For ten shillings you may hire a pony which will take you four miles to the top of the Gap, 700 feet high, and down to the Upper Lake where "luncheon baskets await the tourists". Only ponies or pedestrians are allowed up the Gap. Our car belonged to the Tourish Association and broke the rule. The Gap of Dunloe runs due south. The steep sides of the mountains are covered with enormous boulders left there by a glacier of the Ice Age. Between the rocks are patches of heather and golden broom.

A stream runs down the ravine and drains four mountain tarns. From the top of the Gap is a view of the Upper Lake which goes westwards. Tourists are rowed down the Upper Lake and through the Long Range River to Lake Muckross.

In the Long Range below the Eagle's Nest mountain there is said to be a remarkable four-fold echo of which the last note is louder than the first. From Muckross Lake the boat enters the Lower Lake and lands at Ross Castle some two miles from the town of Killarney.

From the top of the Gap our car turned for home. The Tourist Association are right to keep the road rough. A modern motor road would be out of place. I was never on any of the lakes. I noticed that all the boats were rowing-boats, two-, four- and eight-oared. I was told that down-ward gusts of wind made the lakes dangerous for sail. I saw no steam or motor launches. These would put the oarsmen out of work. Every season a girl pianist from Glasgow takes her place among the oarsmen. This is the first time I ever heard of rowing as an exercise for pianists.

In the morning we motored to the Golf Links. These are laid out along the north shore of the Lower Lake. They are very beautiful and are said to be the best in Europe. In the afternoon we went to the ruins of Muckross Abbey and then into the Demesne. This is now a national park. In the centre is Muckross House, an Elizabethan mansion built of Portland stone. Around it is a famous rock garden. The mansion was empty, but will now be a residence for the Presidents of Ireland. This is as it should be. The hills around the lakes are well wooded with pine, yew and haw-thorn trees. Near the water are bushes of rhododendrons and junipers. Between these is an overgrowth of ferns, fox-gloves, butterwort, harebells, the Rose of Sharon, London Pride, and many other flowers. In the undergrowth was spurge. This is one of the *euphorbiaceae* and the stem when cut exudes a white milky fluid, as from a dandelion. These stems are placed in a bag and bruised with stones. The bag is then sunk into a pool in a river. The fish are paralysed and float to the surface belly upwards. To me this was an entirely novel method of poaching.

Next day I got the train to Mallow, the nearest town to the village of Doneraile. Events in this small village in County Cork had led to two recent libel actions. The first was settled in the High Court at Dublin in 1953. The second was heard in the High Court, London, in 1954. The hearing of this case lasted seven days. The British press published very brief accounts but the Irish papers carried full reports. This case throws light on the working of the Catholic Church in rural Ireland, and is worth recounting here.

Miss Honor Tracy wrote an article entitled "Great Days in the Village". This was published by the *Sunday Times*, London, in their issue of 14th May, 1950. In consequence of this article the parish priest of Doneraile, Canon Maurice O'Connell, brought an action for libel against the *Sunday Times* and Miss Honor Tracy. This action was settled in the High Court, Dublin, in 1951, when the *Sunday Times* apologised to Canon O'Connell and undertook to pay £750 to any charity nominated by him. Counsel for Miss Honor Tracy withdrew from the case. On 8th July, 1951, the *Sunday Times* published the following apology to Canon O'Connell:

Kemsley Newspapers Ltd. tender their apologies to Canon Maurice O'Connell, of Doneraile, Co. Cork, for the publication of an article entitled "Great Days in the Village" which appeared in the *Sunday Times* dated the 14th day of May, 1950, and they express their regret to Canon O'Connell for any injury, damage or inconvenience that the article may have occasioned to him.

They admit that the article constituted an unjustifiable attack upon the character and position of Canon O'Connell, and they unreservedly withdraw the injurious statements and imputations contained in it. To substantiate such withdrawal a sum of £750 will be paid to a charity nominated by Canon O'Connell.

Miss Tracy claimed that the *Sunday Times* libelled her by
publishing this apology and brought an action against them.
This was a libel action within a libel action. Her case was
heard in the High Court, London, before Mr. Justice Glyn-
Jones and a jury of ten men and two women.   I am indebted
to the editor of the *Irish Press* for allowing me to quote passages reported in his newspaper.

> The parish of Doneraile, Co. Cork, was described to the jury
> yesterday (31st March, 1954) when Miss Honor Tracy, author
> and journalist, Sackville Lodge, Gally Hill, Bexhill-on-Sea,
> Sussex, claimed damages for libel against Kemsley Newspapers
> Ltd., publishers of the *Sunday Times.*
>
> Miss Tracy alleged libel in a letter written on behalf of Kems-
> ley Newspapers Ltd. to Mr. Nagle, solicitor for Very Rev.
> Canon Maurice O'Connell, P.P., Doneraile, on April 2nd, 1951,
> and also in an article published on July 8th, 1951, in the *Sunday
> Times.*   The defendants admitted the publication of the libel, but
> pleaded that it was justified.   The Kemsley Newspapers paid
> £750 to the St. Vincent de Paul Society—a charity nominated by
> Canon O'Connell—and published an apology in the *Sunday
> Times* on July 8th, 1951.   Miss Tracy complained that she
> was libelled by the letter offering terms of settlement to Canon
> O'Connell's representatives and by the apology.

The gist of the dispute was that although not mentioned by
name in the article, the village in question was easily identifi-
able as that of Doneraile, Co. Cork, and the events described
were those concerned with the building of a new house for the
parish priest there.   Miss Tracy's contention was that the cost
of building this house (£9,000) was out of all proportion to
the means of the villagers who lived for the most part in a state
of poverty, without running water or electric light.   She also
objected to the means by which this large sum of money was
collected.   She felt that the priest should live like his parishioners and that in any case he already had a pleasant Georgian
house which, so she had been told, he only wished to leave

because he preferred the view he would be able to have from his new house.

Although no names were mentioned in the article the priest in question was recognisable as Canon O'Connell, the parish priest of Doneraile, and he it was who brought the libel action against the *Sunday Times*. Although, as I have said, this action was settled out of court and a full apology made to the Canon by the *Sunday Times*, the whole question was brought up again when Miss Tracy brought her action against the *Sunday Times*, who, she said, had injured her professional career by issuing an apology, thus implying that what she had said in her article was untrue and irresponsible.

The court case depended therefore on the veracity or otherwise of the statements put forward in "Great Days in the Village". The suggestion that the new house was built merely so that the Canon could have a good view was raised by Mr. Paull when he was cross-examining Miss Tracy for the *Sunday Times*.

Mr. Paull: Do you think the attack you made in the article was a fair attack on Canon O'Connell?

Miss Tracey: I thought it was a fair criticism. One of the facts that annoyed the Canon when he was living in the old house was the noise caused by the children playing in the streets and also the shaggy donkeys walking around the village. He wanted to get away from all that.

Mr. Paull: Are you suggesting that the Canon was spending £9,000 building a house to get one with a view?

Miss Tracy: It means that the Canon wanted to get out of the main street of Doneraile.

Mr. Paull: You cannot say worse about a priest than that, merely because he didn't like the view from his house, he spent £9,000 on a new one.

Miss Tracy: I thought it was wrong. We are dealing with an Irish priest and the priests in Ireland are very different from the priests in England. The parish priest in Ireland will suit himself in all matters.

In the course of the evidence it became clear that the figure of £9,000 was incorrect and that the house did in fact cost about £7,000. Canon O'Connell had said that the first two estimates for the building of the house had been turned down by his Bishop (the Bishop of Cloyne) as being too high. In evidence, Canon O'Connell said that he had had the house built on the order of his Bishop, and as he himself was over 80, this work was undertaken not so much for himself as for future generations of parish priests. He agreed that the overall cost of building the new house and repairing the old one (which was now to house two curates) came to just over £7,000. As he had earlier named the figure as £4,000 he was questioned about this and replied:

"I gave the defence the figure of £4,000 in an off-hand way. I did not bother to go into details."

"Would you call 'about £7,000' about £4,700?"

Canon O'Connell: "About £4,700 is a loose way of saying it."

Earlier in the case the question of the method by which the money had been collected was raised. In her evidence, Miss Tracy said that the Canon was in the custom of reading out the list of subscriptions in church, starting with the largest and working his way down to the smallest. This, she felt was a form of moral blackmail and compelled the villagers to give more than they could afford. She also stated:

"When the Canon appealed for money, I noticed a considerable change in his voice. I had considerable difficulty in hearing the sermon but none whatever in hearing him appeal for money."

She was asked if any of the villagers had complained about the amount of money they were expected to subscribe, and she said that several of them had grumbled to her, prefacing their remarks with "Mind, you didn't have it from me" and "Mind, I didn't say it". Someone had said, "All he'll be needing now is a swimming-pool."

On the question of dues collected at Doneraile, it appeared that four a year were collected as opposed to the two usually collected at Christmas and Easter in the Catholic Church, but that in one year five dues were collected, the fifth being exclusively for the new house. This was later denied by Canon O'Connell.

During the seven days' hearing a great deal more evidence of the same sort was heard, much of it contradictory, and in his summing-up the judge said:

"What is really said by Miss Tracy is this: The majority of the parishioners in this parish—yes, and in many other parishes in the twenty-six counties—are desperately poor, poorly housed, lacking proper sanitation, and electric light. They don't have to consider whether thay have any cigarettes: they can't even afford meat.

"In these circumstances, she thought that for the Catholic Church to be continually pricking these people to pay, pay, pay, so that the clergy may enjoy a standard of living so much better than the people's, was wrong. She thought that to build a new house in Doneraile when the parishioners could not even afford meat was wrong."

But although the judge advised the jury to treat all Miss Tracy's statements as having been given in absolute sincerity. the evidence for her allegations was not very strong and in many instances was founded on hearsay.

The jury took more than five hours to reach a decision—almost a record for a libel case—finally awarding Miss Tracy £500 in respect of the letter written on behalf of Kemsley Newspapers Ltd. to Mr. Nagle, solicitor in Ireland for the Very Rev. Maurice Canon O'Connell, P.P., and a further £2,500 for the apology published in the *Sunday Times* on July 8th, 1951, concerning her article "Great Days in the Village".

CHAPTER XI

I am Assaulted at Mallow

AT Mallow I went to the Central Hotel. Bed and breakfast 14s. I at once inquired about transport to Doneraile. The town and the village are on the same bus route, but the only bus to Doneraile was at 7.30 p.m. and the bus from Doneraile arrived at 8.30 a.m. I would have to find accommodation at Doneraile. Fortunately two friends of Mr. Eoin O'Mahony called at the hotel that Thursday afternoon. One friend was Mr. John D. Sullivan, solicitor, who invited me to lunch the next day. After lunch we would motor to Doneraile, and our party would include Mrs. Clark, the Mallow reporter for the *Cork Examiner*. My second visitor was Major O'Regan, who invited me to dinner on Saturday evening. His estate is on the banks of the Blackwater River near the town. He had been British Military Attaché at Madrid in 1946. After dinner he showed me the Official Spanish History of the Civil War. The pity is that it has never been translated into English.

On the Friday afternoon we motored to Doneraile which is nine miles north-east of Mallow. Our road went through the village of Buttevant where I saw the steeple of the church. It is four miles from the steeple of the church at Doneraile. Between these two steeples at the beginning of last century was run the first steeplechase. We then went some five miles east of our way to look for Kilcolman Castle. This castle with 3,000 acres of land was given by Elizabeth I to Edward Spenser in 1586. The place had previously belonged to the attainted Earl of Desmond. Here Spenser wrote the *Faerie Queene*. The castle was burnt by the Irish in 1598 during the Earl of

Tyrone's Rebellion. Spenser escaped but one of his children was burnt to death in the fire. "That was not the fault of the Irish," said an Irish parish priest to me. I did not argue this nice point of moral theology. For twenty minutes we sped along secondary roads and through country lanes. Then I said to my companions who were discussing the whereabouts of the castle, "We've passed it."

"Where?"

"A mile ago we passed a farm. Next the farm was an ivy-covered keep. That was the only ancient monument in sight. It must have been the castle."

They did not reply but the car proceeded to Doneraile. A Georgian house was the largest in this clean village. In that house Canon Sheehan had written his novels. He was a very considerable novelist. His greatest work is *The Triumph of Failure*. This was translated into German and in Germany six editions were published. Many of the houses were cottages and the occupants got water from a tap in the street. One was quite derelict and I asked a man in the street:

"When was this last occupied?"

"No one has lived there since twenty years. It's been condemned by the County Council."

We then went to the public-house kept by Mr. Mannix, in the main street. It was partly a pub and a shop, but it had electric light and indoor sanitation. Mr. Mannix was ill and I did not see him, but I saw Miss Mannix who had been a governess in Spain for twenty years and spoke Spanish fluently. She was non-committal about the events that had made the village famous.

From there we motored to Canon O'Connell's new house, a modern villa outside and above the village. On each pier of the gate was a round stone ball. I am told that in feudal times these stone balls were a warning that the Lord of the Manor had the right to execute persons who incurred his displeasure. On learning the object of my visit the Canon asked, "Would you like to see the bedrooms?"

"No, no, Canon, obviously this is not a palace. I was interested by your refusal to allow Mrs. Preece to arrange for a dance."

"The Hunt Committee had agreed that no dance would be held without my permission. When Mrs. Preece asked me I refused permission. It was to be an all-night dance. There are too many. People should be in bed by twelve o'clock. It may be all right in cities where there are lights. Here there are dark country lanes."

"In cities there are motor-cars. In your evidence, Canon, taken on commission, you said it would be bad for discipline that the two curates should live with you."

"Familiarity breeds contempt. In the army a colonel does not hob-nob with his subalterns. Each curate has his own house and housekeeper. He pays for both out of his stipend. In Ireland it's the boys who sit at the top of the class who enter the Church. They could make more money in any profession or in commerce."

"What is the stipend of a curate?"

The Canon did not reply. So I thanked him for his courtesy in seeing me and said good-bye. The Canon was 85. I could have told him that in England, Scotland and Wales the curates live with the parish priest and have free board and lodging. In addition they have a stipend of forty pounds a year, and usually a share of the Christmas and Easter Offerings. In England a curate could earn ten times his stipend as an unskilled labourer. An Irish priest after a three weeks' visit to London declared: "I'm appalled by the penury of the English clergy." He must have been more appalled by the penury of Our Lord.

We then went to Doneraile Court, a mansion standing in its own grounds. The large hall is lit from a cupola, and from the hall a beautiful staircase, visible all the way, ascends to the third floor. In the spacious days of old this home would have employed at least a dozen servants. We had tea with Lord and Lady Doneraile in the ground-floor drawing-room where mullion windows overlook the lawns and woods. Lord Doneraile before he succeeded to the title was a sheep farmer in New Zealand where he married. There are no children.

After tea Lord Doneraile showed me his workroom. This was a room to the right of the entrance. One eighth of the room was partitioned by a curtain. Behind the curtain a stair led down to a door which gave entrance from the yard. Up these stairs the Doneraile Freemasons used to go for the weekly meeting of their Lodge. One night when they were all in the room a slight noise was heard behind the curtain. The Masons investigated and found behind the curtain the Honourable Elizabeth St. Leger, a daughter of the house. She had heard their secrets. So they made her a Mason. I used to think she was the only woman Mason, but I heard a similar story of a girl who lived in a large house near Queenstown.

Once a Mason, always a Mason. I was made a Mason in 1916 at the Pembroke Dock Lodge, but have not practised Masonry since 1920. In that year I was received into the Catholic Church which forbids its members to practise Masonry. Rome does not distinguish between British and Continental Masons. I say British because Lodge Number One is in Scotland. British Masonry is Christian. One of its highest Lodges is the Lodge of the Holy Trinity. British Masonry is monarchist. Continental Masonry is atheistic and anti-monarchist. It is said to have aided the French Revolution, and certainly it had a sinister part in the Spanish Civil War of 1936. In the middle of the last century the Grand Lodge of England broke with the Grand Orient, which governs Continental Masonry. Many Catholics have as queer ideas about British Masons as Protestants hold about Jesuits. A Jesuit is behind every curtain or lurking round the nearest corner. They invented the immoral maxim, now so popular, that the end justifies the means. In point of fact the sum of 100 Rhenish guilders awaits the person who can prove to the satisfaction of the Faculty of Law at the Universities of Heidelberg or of Bonn that any Jesuit ever sponsored or defended that maxim. So also many Catholics regard British Freemasons as conspirators engaged in plots and stratagems, whereas in reality they are honest folk mostly from the middle classes. They are attracted to Masonry by its symbolism. They are generous people and look after the widows and orphans of fellow Masons.

The Catholic Church objects to secret societies, or perhaps it would be more accurate to say that the Church objects to non-Catholic secret societies, because there are several Catholic secret societies. In Britain we have the Catenians. Membership of this society is limited to some of the laity. More democratic are the Knights of St. Columba. In the United States of America a similar society is called the Knights of Columbus, and in Australia is the very secret Knights of the Southern Cross. Men who join any of these societies are expected to do so for the same reason that other men become Freemasons—the desire to help their fellows. Of course some will join any society or political party not for what they can give but for what they can get out of it.

When the member of a secret society is also a member of some public authority and has to decide on the most suitable candidate for any post he should vote for the Masonic or for the Catholic candidate as the case may be, provided other things are equal between the candidates. Unfortunately he may vote in this way when other things are not equal, and this is what brings secret societies into disrepute.

Next day, Saturday, I received at the hotel an out-of-date Irish newspaper. It was tied with string and came by post. On the front page there was no indication of the whereabouts of the paragraph in which I might be interested. Never send

an unmarked newspaper to anyone unless he be your greatest
enemy. He may then have the trouble of reading the entire
paper without finding anything of particular interest. When
I got to the middle page of this newspaper a letter fell out. It
was written on the pay-in slips of a Bank, and advised me to
visit a ruined chapel forty miles distant. I could not decipher
the signature and I call the writer the Antiquarian. He sent
me five similar letters all wrapped in old newspapers. Had
I followed his advice I would have spent the rest of my life
exploring ancient ruins in County Cork. His newspapers
were stamped at the rate for printed matter, and I like to think
that the Bank supplied not only the pay-in slips but also the
pen and ink. He reminded me of the Scotsman whom I
called McQuilternach in *Arches of the Years*.

On Sunday night I was talking to Mr. John D. Sullivan,
the solicitor, in the larger writing-room of the hotel. We
were discussing the Irish character. Mr. Sullivan said that
the wild Irishman, the man who kicked a tray out of the but-
ler's hands and scattered the glasses to the four corners of the
room, belonged to the era of Handy Andy and the novels of
Charles Lever. He had gone for good. He might exist in
England or in the U.S.A., but not in Ireland. Suddenly we
heard a crash, and my companion remarked that people had no
right to be larking in the hotel at that hour of the night. It
was 11 p.m. We were alone in the writing-room. The
door opened and a chauffeur popped his head into the room:
"Someone's gone mad and is wrecking the hotel." He withdrew. Next moment the door was thrown open by a young
man, tall and broad-shouldered. He glared at us.

"Sit down and take it easy," said Mr. Sullivan.

For reply the young man kicked a chair which fell beside
me. He then seized another chair and banged it on the floor
beside me. I repeated the invitation to sit down and take it
easy, but the young man came nearer. I then rose and said,
"There's a Guard behind you." He turned to the guard who

had just entered the room. What they said I did not hear, but the Guard left the room followed by Mr. Sullivan. My exit was barred by the chairs and the young man. So I retreated to the end of the writing-table. The young man then rushed at me and gave me a push that sent me to the other side of the room where I fell violently into a desk-chair. I then left the room and saw other visitors standing by their bed-room doors. Three Guards then came up the stairs, entered the writing-room, and took the young man away. I returned to the writing-room and a few minutes later a Guard re-appeared. I told him of the assault but added, "I make no complaint because I do not wish to be detained here as a witness." The guard withdrew and I went to bed.

I woke next morning to find that my four lower right ribs were badly bruised. So far as I could ascertain none were broken. After breakfast I went to Mr. Sullivan's office and instructed him to claim ten guineas for the assault. He said I had a cast-iron case and that ten guineas was merely nominal. I replied that I was not prepared to return from England to claim more. I did not think my ribs were broken, but might have an X-ray in Dublin. If they were broken I would go into hospital. In that case I would claim £50 per week from Lloyd's Insurance. That would complicate the case which I hoped would be settled for ten guineas. It was. I returned to the hotel where I saw the Superintendent of Police who asked me to be at the court at 11 a.m. the next day.

The following account of the proceedings is taken from the *Evening Herald,* Dublin, of 10th May and from the *Cork Examiner* of 11th May, 1955. So far as I know the only British newspaper to report the case was the *Manchester Guardian*.

ALLEGED ASSAULT ON NOTED AUTHOR
INCIDENT IN MALLOW HOTEL

At Mallow District Court yesterday before Mr. H. L. Connor, D. J., Edward Footte, Newberry, Mallow, was charged with an assault on Dr. Halliday Sutherland, a visitor to the hotel and well-known author; with an assault on Sergt. Daniel Aherne, Garda Siochana, and with malicious damage to property at the Central Hotel, Mallow, on the 8th of May.

Mr. P. J. O'Driscoll, solr., represented the defendant and Mr. J. B. Sullivan appeared for an interested party.

Supt. P. Kelly, Mallow, prosecuting, said that at 11 p.m. on Sunday night last he entered the Central Hotel, Mallow, with some other people whilst a bridge tournament was in progress. Dr. Halliday Sutherland, a resident at the hotel, was assaulted by accused who also broke some furniture. But for the fact that the chair over which he was thrown was heavily upholstered, Dr. Sutherland would have sustained very heavy injuries.

Supt. Kelly asked that the case be adjourned for a fortnight, after the evidence of Dr. Sutherland had been taken in order not to delay him in this country.

"GONE MAD"

Dr. Sutherland said he was in the writing-room at about 11 o'clock when somebody opened the door and said: "Somebody is gone mad and is wrecking the hotel."

Shortly afterwards, Footte entered the room. He kicked a chair and it fell at witness's feet. "I said to him," said Dr. Sutherland, "take it easy, sit down." He did not sit down. A Civic Guard came in and I said to the accused, "There is a Guard behind you." Something passed between the Guard and the accused and the Guard then left and I was left alone with the accused.

I moved to the end of the table and he followed me. He then rushed at me and put his hands on my shoulders and I was thrown backwards on a desk-chair, the arms of which were heavily bound with leather, and I bruised my lower ribs on the right side. I then went out of the room and saw three Guards come up the stairs and enter the room.

APOLOGY OFFERED

Mr. P. J. O'Driscoll, solicitor, said he wanted to express on behalf of Footte his sincere apologies for the incident and he asked if Dr. Sutherland said he was prepared to accept the apologies.

Mr. O'Driscoll: In view of the apologies are you prepared to forget the incident?

Justice: How could he forget it?

Dr. Sutherland: I have been trying to forget the pain in my side. I am here writing a book *Irish Journey*, and the incident has certainly given me material for it.

When Dr. Sutherland said that, he thought the man was insane at the time of the incident.

Mr. O'Driscoll: You thought he was insane at the time and you have medical experience?

Witness: I had experience for six months as a medical officer in a lunatic asylum.

No other witnesses were examined and the case was adjourned to the next court on May 24.

After the hearing Justice Connor entertained me to lunch, and then motored me to the station where I got the train to Dublin.

The case was next heard on Tuesday, 12th July, and I quote the following report from *The Kerryman* of 16th July, 1955:

MALLOW COURT
SUCCESSFUL PLEA OF TEMPORARY INSANITY

It was unfortunate that the District Court had no jurisdiction on the question of insanity or lunacy, and the right thing to do would be to return the defendant for a jury, and the jury could then find on the plea of insanity, said District Justice Connor at Mallow on Tuesday, when Edward Footte, farmer, Newberry, Mallow, was successful in his plea of temporary insanity on the occasion of assault stated to have been committed in a Mallow hotel on the night of Sunday, May 8.

Footte was charged with assaulting Dr. Halliday Sutherland, the English author, and Sergt. Daniel Aherne, of the Garda Siochana. He was also charged with being drunk and disorderly and with damaging the property of the hotel.

Supt. P. Kelly, who prosecuted, said the case had been before the court at a previous hearing, and Mr. O'Driscoll, solr., for Footte, had submitted that the defendant was temporarily insane.

Justice: Mr. O'Driscoll raised the point about insanity and quoted a decision of the House of Lords on the matter, and the charge was adjourned. Unless the State can show something to rebut that I am afraid I will have to hold with Mr. O'Driscoll.

Supt. Kelly: The defendant did not give evidence himself the last day.

Justice: No! But Mr. O'Driscoll made a submission and Dr. Halliday Sutherland gave evidence to the effect that the defendant was insane at the time.

Supt. Kelly: Are you prepared to accept that evidence without the defendant's evidence?

"ABSOLUTELY SURE"

Justice: Dr. Sutherland was most clear about it. The case quoted by Mr. O'Driscoll was that drunkenness was one thing and insanity another. Dr. Sutherland was very clear. He is an expert, of course, and he said he was absolutely sure that the man was insane at the time.

Supt Kelly: You are, of course, entitled to convict for drunkenness.

Mr. O'Driscoll said he had intended to raise a point on that. At the last hearing he had pleaded guilty of drunkenness but not to being drunk and disorderly, because the disorder arose from insanity.

"SIMPLE DRUNKENNESS"

The Justice said he would strike out 'disorderly behaviour' and he would fine the defendant on simple drunkenness.

Mr. O'Driscoll said that, under Section 12 of the Act, a fine of 10s. was the maximum fine that could be imposed.

Supt. Kelly said there was also a charge of damage to the property of the hotel, and he submitted that the defendant was liable on that.

The Justice said he understood the defence to say, on the last occasion, that defendant had made arrangements with the hotel about the damage.

The Justice said that 10s. was the maximum fine allowed for drunkenness and he would impose that.

The general conduct of the defendant justified an order binding him over. He would order the defendant to enter into a bond to be of good behaviour for a period of two years on two solvent sureties of £25 or one of £50.

So it would seem that the solitary witness for the prosecution had also been the expert medical witness for the defence!

After this sad story I shall now tell you of the seasoned Australian of whom I heard in Melbourne. It is the story of a morning headache.

The patient, a Melbourne man, complains of morning headaches. "Nothing organically wrong," says the Collins Street physician, "but blood pressure is a little up, tongue slightly furred, fine tremor of hands; conjuctivae are somewhat congested, and knee jerks a trifle brisk; Babinski is negative, and Von Quincke positive. A case of Functional Remittent Matudinal Cephalgia. What about alchohol?"

"Not more than the next man, doctor, but I admit I drink at meals."

"Then we must go further afield to discover the little something whose adjustment will restore the balance of our metabolism. Tell me all about your average day."

"Well, doctor, for me one day is mostly the same as another. I lead a very regular life. For a start I get up at seven and to shift the headache have a couple of stiff whiskies. After that I don't have another drink until I've shaved. Fact is I feel a bit weak after shaving. A psycho-analyst once told me I had the Delilah-Samson Complex, but when he explained what that meant I knew he was crackers. Then there's breakfast. Now when I said I drink at meals, I didn't mean at breakfast. All I have is tea or coffee. Cocoa makes me sick."

"After breakfast I set out for the office. On the way I look in at the local and have one for the road. At the office I read letters, dictate replies, and generally see to my business. At eleven I pop round the corner and have a sniffter with the boys. We discuss the racing news. Then there's lunch and as I told you, I admit I do drink at meals.

"Back to my office for interviews with prospective clients. These people expect a glass or two of port. I think they drink too much but of course it's good for business. Then there's letters to be signed and all the work of clearing up for the day. At five I go round the corner and join the boys. Of course we have a few rounds of drinks—depends on how many we are.

"Dinner at seven is at home, and my wife likes punctuality. So I leave the boys at six as soon as the pub closes. My wife likes a drink and we usually have a couple of whiskies before dinner. That woman drinks too much. Then comes dinner and, as I told you, I admit I do drink at meals. Afterwards we may go to the pictures, perhaps once a week, but I prefer a quiet evening at home. That's how it is most nights, and I'll have eight or nine whiskies, ending of course with a night-cap. Always in bed by eleven. Well, doctor, that's been my life since the Second World War—a very regular life. Some might call it monotonous, but I don't find it so."

"And except for the headaches, you feel fit? Is that what you say? Is that what you're telling me?"

"Well, to be quite frank—and it's no use being anything else with a doctor—I don't think my nerves are as steady as they were at Alamein—but that's got nothing to do with my work. It's this way. My wife and I live in a new suburb. They say the houses were built on the site of an old rubbish dump. Anyway, the whole district is infested. The M.O.H. ought to do something about it. That's the way bubonic plague gets around. I suppose we all have our own secret phobias and mine's bubonic plague. Even to think of it gives me the willies or the jitters and I'd go screwy unless I kept a firm grip on myself. So when they come into the house I get cracking with the old revolver. I don't profess to be a first-class shot. No, doctor, I'm not a good shot and you'll find a little astigmatism in my right eye but, even when I miss, the noise scares them away. The wife says it scares the neighbours also. Now without claiming to be what you might call a religious man, I try to follow the Good Book when it says 'Thou shalt love thy neighbour as thyself'. Yes, Love is certainly sublime. Very sublime. But I tell that woman—and the last time I tell her is at 2 a.m. this morning when I fired from the bed—I tell her that if our neighbours had a proper sense of civic responsibility and put down as much poison as we put down there would not be a rat within a mile of the house.

"And that reminds me I've brought along the two I shot last night. In the moonlight I saw them moving slowly over the carpet. I fired from the bed. If you find they're infected you could write to the M.O.H. He'd likely pay more attention to you than to me. Holy Snakes! Are you ill, doctor? Steady! Heavens, the doctor's fainted!"

CHAPTER XII

The Story of the Captain

ON Saturday, May 14th, I travelled from Dublin to Cork in an express Diesel-engined corridor train. The Irish Government had kindly given me a pass on their railways and motor-coaches. At Cork a taxi took me some four hundred yards from the station to the Hotel Metropole. The taxi-driver was a fat smiling pink-faced bucolic Irishman. He said the fare was 3s. I gave him 3s. 6d. Later the hall porter in the hotel told me the fare was 1s. 6d. The Metropole, bed and breakfast 22s. 6d., is a comfortable hotel with radio in every bedroom. When the American couple in the next room placed six pence in the slot and turned on the radio I could hear the whole programme without expense. The walls were not soundproof. The cashier told me that three of the waitresses were leaving for England where as factory hands they could earn more money.

The city of Cork lies in the valley of the Lee and on the surrounding hills. Through the river quite large steamers are able to reach the docks in the centre of the city, fifteen miles from Cork Harbour. In the lower part of the city many of the main streets are built on piles. Otherwise this part of the city might have looked like Amsterdam.

On Sunday I heard Mass at St. Patrick's. Here as in every church I attended in Eire there was no collection. There was a plate in the portico to which those entering contributed coppers. I lunched that day with Professor Denis Gwynn whom I had known in London thirty years ago when he edited the *Catholic Times*.

After lunch Professor Gwynn motored me to the Protestant Grammar School where I had tea with the headmaster, the Rev. Mr. Burrough and his wife. The other guest was Bishop Simms, the Protestant Bishop of Cork. We had a pleasant tea and it was obvious that in the south of Ireland there are friendly relations between Protestants and Catholics. Bishop Simms, as he drove me back to the Metropole, said there were 5,000 Protestants and 70,000 Catholics in the City of Cork.

Next day I met Mr. Tom Crosbie, one of the proprietors of the *Cork Examiner*, who took me to lunch at the Rotary Club where we heard an interesting paper by a girl who had crossed the Atlantic in a ketch. After lunch Mr. Crosbie motored me fifteen miles along the right bank of the river Lee to the Royal Munster Yacht Club on the western shore of Cork Harbour, one of the largest natural harbours in the world. From the windows of this flourishing yacht club I saw the two great islands in the harbour. The nearest and largest was Spike Island. This was once a British convict prison, where convicts awaited transportation to Australia. More recently political offenders were detained here. Only one of them ever escaped. He now owns a confectioner's shop in O'Connell Street, Dublin. The other island is Haulbowline, once a Royal Naval establishment. It is now mostly occupied by a steel works, but at one end the Irish Navy have a small establishment, where officers entertained me at their Mess later in the week.

Beyond the islands I could see Cobh, once known as Queenstown. Here is the club house of the Royal Cork Yacht Club, the oldest in the world. It began in 1720 as the Haulbowline Sailing Club. The Commodore of this club is known as "The Admiral". By permission of the Lords of the Admiralty he has the right to fly as his burgee a Union Jack with an Irish Harp in the centre. It is curious that the Irish who have altered the names of Queenstown and Kingstown should still retain the adjective Royal. When I visited this club there were few members. They missed the Royal

Navy. Indeed all the people of Cobh missed the Navy. An empty part of the harbour is still called the Destroyer Anchorage. It must have meant much to this small town when a flotilla of destroyers cast anchor there. Today only two British liners, the *Mauritania* and the *Britannia*, cast anchor off Cobh on their voyages to and from New York.

From Cork I went for two days to Cobh, pronounced Cove, a small town of over 5,000 people on the most southern of three islands on the east side of Cork Harbour, one of the safest natural harbours in the world. These three islands are separated by narrow channels that are easily crossed by rail and by road bridges. Cobh is fifteen miles from the City of Cork and by rail the journey takes half an hour. Kingstown near Dublin is now called Dun Laoghaire, pronounced *Dun Leary*, and the old name of Queenstown has now been changed to Cobh.

My hosts at Cobh were Mrs. Buckley and her son, who are proprietors of the Westbourne Hotel which stands on the front facing the harbour. One of the first questions I put to Mr. Buckley was: "Did you know Captain Burns?"

"You mean the old sea captain. Why, yes, he and his wife stayed at our hotel until they found a house at Rushbrook. That's the next station. It used to be a very select residential area—retired naval and army officers with a sprinkling of retired civil servants. Something like your Cheltenham. One day the Protestant Rector called at the hotel, but the Captain was out for a walk. The Rector asked me if the Captain had been Royal Navy or Merchant Service. I did not know, but on his return I told the Captain. He cupped his hands to his mouth and said in a loud whisper: 'The bastard. That's the sort of question he would ask.' I didn't think the Captain had any religion. All the same he was a very decent man. He is now dead and Burns was not his name."

I first heard of the Captain from a Cork business man:

"My wife and I were living at Rushbrook when the Cap-

tain and his wife got a house there. On week-days I went
every morning to Cork by train. One morning I missed the
train. Outside the station stood the Captain's car with himself at the wheel. The bonnet was pointed in the direction of
Cork. So I took a chance and went up to him: 'I've missed
my train, sir, and if you're going to Cork I'd be very grateful
for a lift.' He turned and stared at me. He was thick-set,
clean-shaven, pink complexion, strong features, large grey
eyes, bushy eyebrows, and grey hair. Then he shouted:
'Thank God someone in this blasted place has a tongue in his
head. Step on board, mister, and I'll land you at Cork.'
That was the beginning of a friendship which lasted until he
died. Every week my wife and I visited his house and he
with his wife came to ours. Since his teens he had sailed the
Seven Seas. He was the most entertaining man I ever met.
He was shrewd, too, as you may judge from what he told me
about Prohibition in the United States:

"'I was then in command of an ocean-going tramp, 10,000
tons, three holds, one forward, two aft. We were at Montreal
taking cargo for New York. It was a Tuesday morning when
the agents brought me a cable from the owners at Liverpool.
I was to sail next morning, discharge at New York, and pick up
a new cargo for Pernambuco. At noon the dockers had finished
loading. All the holds were full, except for about three feet in
the back hold aft. I looked at the vacant space and then asked
the Chief Engineer to come to my cabin.

"'Chief, would you like to share in 300 per cent profit?'

"'It canna be done, Captain.'

"'Of course it can. If you buy a bottle of Scotch for about
one dollar and sell it for four, that's a profit of 300 per cent.'

"'It's naething of the kind. It's a profit of 75 per cent.'

"'How do you make that out?'

"'Well, for every 100 dollars ye get, ye've spent 25. That
leaves ye a profit of 75 per cent.'

"'See here, if I buy something for one penny and sell it to

143

you for 100 pounds, am I not making a profit of 2,339 per cent?'

"'No, ye're not. Out of the 100 pounds ye've spent $\frac{1}{2400}$ of a penny. That means a profit of 99·999 per cent. I canna be fashed carrying the decimals further.'

"'Well, are you interested in making 75 per cent?'

"'Aye, if it's honest.'

"'It's as honest as the day'—and I told him my plans.

"I went ashore to the agents: 'I'm sailing at 3 p.m. unless you've more cargo.'

"'Not very likely, Captain. What space is left?'

"'About 3,700 cubic feet in the after hold. I'll be on board at 2 p.m. for signing.'

"Then I went into the city and called on a wholesale whisky merchant whom I knew: 'Can you supply 200 cases of proprietary Scotch out of bond for export?'

"'Yes. Who's the buyer?'

"'Manuel Garcia, 3 Grand Via, Pernambuco.'

"'Is he known to us?'

"'No, but I suppose you'll take my cheque?'

"'Of course I will, and many thanks for getting us the order.'

"'Then you'd better phone the ship's agents, and find out what's the freight. I'll give you the cheque.'

"The wholesalers telephoned. The agents accepted the cargo, and quoted the freight. They would send a messenger with the necessary papers at once. The wholesaler promised to have the cargo alongside the ship by 2.30 p.m. at the latest. I then gave the wholesaler my cheque for 10,800 dollars."

"'Do you want receipts?'

"'No, no, post the documents in the usual way to Garcia.'

"From there I went to the leading hotel in Montreal and asked for an American whom I had never met. Soon I saw the bell-boy and a tall, elegant young man, clean-shaven, with tinted spectacles. He smiled pleasantly: 'You wish to see me, Captain?'

"'Yes, for a moment.'

"'Well, come into the smoking-room.'

"We entered, and sat down in a quiet corner of the room. Then I said: 'You want whisky?'

"He stared at me in blank astonishment: 'I never touch the stuff.'

"'Maybe you know those who do.'

"He looked even more astonished and smiled: 'Say, Captain, I reckon you've got hold of the wrong man.'

"'I'm sorry to have troubled you'—and I rose to go.

"'Sit down.' This was said not in a pleasant but in a raspy voice, but I obeyed.

"'What brand?'

"'Scotch proprietary.'

"'How much?'

"'Two hundred cases.'

"'You deliver?'

"'No, you collect.'

"'When?'

"'Friday night, 10 p.m.'

"'Where?'

"I gave him the latitude and longitude. These he noted in a small pocket-book: 'Where's that?'

"'Ten miles off the coast of Maine.'

"'You keep far out. Suppose it's too rough for the launches?'

"'Then I go on.'

"'You don't wait?'

"'No.'

"'Can I inspect the stuff?'

"'No, but you can see it being loaded at the docks under Customs' supervision between 2 and 3 p.m. today.'

"'How much per case?'

"'Hundred and fifty dollars. If your launches meet us, only one man will be allowed on board. He should have the money, 30,000 dollars. After payment, the cargo will be delivered.'

"'Why, Captain, you just think of everything. Well, good-bye, and I hope we meet again.'

"I returned to the ship where I saw the Chief Engineer. He gave me his cheque for 5,400 dollars. This I sent to England by air mail. At 2.30 p.m. I watched our cargo coming on board. Among the few spectators on the quay I noticed the young and elegantly dressed American. He was accompanied by a seafaring man.

"Next day we were out of the St. Laurence and steaming south. In the north I saw a ship coming our way. She was burning plenty of coal. As soon as she was over the horizon I had a look at her with the glass. She was high in the water and looked like a ship I had seen in Montreal Harbour. That ship had flown the Stars and Stripes, but this ship flew no flag.

"When she was a mile astern a flash-lamp twinkled from her bridge. The message was: Stop your engines. I sent for the Chief Engineer and told him what I'd seen.

"'What do you make of it, Captain?'

"'I think it's got to do with that dapper young American. I think she's a pirate.'

"'What are ye going to do, Captain?'

"'I'm going half-speed. That will bring her up all the sooner. Keep all your men below. The crew will stay in the fo'c'sle.'

"At that moment Sparks, rather breathless, came to me: 'Captain, that ship astern is in distress. She is morsing us to stop our engines. What are you going to do?'

"'I'll tell you what you're going to do, Mister. You go back to the wireless cabin and don't touch the wireless. When that ship comes abeam, you will be down on the deck away from your post; you see, a bullet might splinter the glass.'

"He looked amazed but did as he was told. The bosun told the crew to stay in the fo'c'sle and to stand clear of the ports. I went to the bridge where I put the telegraph at half-speed. Then I told the third officer and the steersman: 'Lash the helm.

As the ship astern comes abeam, go into the chartroom and shelter under the table. If a bullet hits one of the ports the glass may splinter and give you a nasty cut.'

"Then I went to the bows and entered the tarpaulin that covered the twelve-pounder. Where or when I got that gun is no one's business, but I was R.N.R. and the gun had done useful service in the First World War. I got under the tarpaulin and loaded the gun. Then I waited. Soon the other ship was abeam and within three hundred yards. Her skipper shouted through a megaphone: 'Stop your engines.'

"My ship made no reply and continued on her course like the Flying Dutchman. The man put down his megaphone, picked up a sub-machine-gun, and sprayed our bridge. I heard the ping of bullets on the steel superstructure. The crash of glass meant that at least one port had been hit. Then I fired. I had aimed at the funnel but the shell carried away the steam pipe to his siren. A moment later his upper-deck was covered by a cloud of steam. The pirate had the heart of a chick ten or eleven days old. He turned off to starboard. I had another shot at the funnel. This time the shell blew a hole at the foot. His after-deck was covered with black smoke and steam. An untidy mess that he trailed after him as he returned to the north. I cleaned the gun, fixed the tarpaulin, and went to the bridge. The chartroom was covered with broken glass. Under the table the third officer and the steersman were unhurt. I told them to unlash the wheel and continue course. The third officer appeared to be rather excited: 'That was Piracy on the High Seas. You'll report him, Captain?'

"'Take a look at the other ship. Am I to report that I blew away a steam pipe and made a hole in his funnel? Forget it ever happened, Mister.'

"The steersman grinned. He had sailed with me in the war.

"On Friday night I took the precaution to have a hosepipe laid out on the port side. The sea was calm. At nine-thirty I saw ahead the lights of four launches. As we came up to them I stopped the engines. One launch used a flash-lamp and morsed: 'Put your lights out.' For reply I ordered all deck lights to be put on, also the searchlight. That dazzled them. Then I took up the megaphone and called: 'Landing launch to make fast on the port side aft. Others to stand clear.' The launch came alongside and was made fast. Then I ordered the water to be turned on. Two seamen held the nozzle of the hose and directed the jet outwards and over the launch. Then I called through the megaphone; 'I am lowering a Jacob's ladder. Only the boss is to come on board. Any who attempt to follow will get the hose.' The searchlight showed six men in the cockpit. They consulted, and then one of them came up the ladder. The Chief and I awaited him on deck. As soon as he pushed his head above the rail I saw the ugliest face that ever escaped the electric chair at Sing-Sing. He snarled: 'Why the hell don't you obey orders. I said Lights Out.'

"'To hell with your orders. I'm the one who gives orders here. I take them from no one. Got the money?'

"'How much whisky have you?'

"'Brother, you'd better go down the ladder. You're just wasting time, and I'm sailing in thirty seconds.'

"'You win,' he said, and the Chief and I helped him to land on deck. He was half blinded by the searchlight. Two of the crew pulled up the ladder. The hose was turned off. 'Follow the Chief,' I said.

"The Chief led the way to the saloon which was under the bridge. The hoodlum followed, I brought up the rear. I noticed the bulge in his side pockets. He was a two-gun man. The Chief and I had only one each. In the saloon I gave him the chair at the top of the table. I sat at the side of the table.

"'Where's the other guy?' he asked.

"'He's behind you. At the door. Just to see there's no funny business. Now I want 30,000 dollars.'

"'You don't trust me?'

"'No, brother, sad to say I don't trust any of you. But you trust us, brother, so everything is on the up and up.'

"From his breast pocket he pulled a pile of notes, and counted them out. They were genuine. I put the notes in the safe in my cabin which opened off the saloon. Then we all went aft to watch the unloading. The hoodlum wanted fifty cases in each launch. We lowered five cases at a time. Three of the crew fitted the slings. Two others manned the guide-ropes to the derrick. Another worked the winch. The second officer supervised the work. The first officer was on the bridge. When the fourth launch was made fast, the hoodlum said he would board her. I thought he was wise. His friends might have sailed without him. The third officer had the hose full on and two of the crew lowered the ladder. The Hoodlum left without a word. The ladder up and the water off we lowered the rest of the cargo. That was the end of it. The whole business had taken one-and-a-half hours.

"The Chief and I went to my cabin where we decided the bonus of the crew. Every man on board was to get 10 dollars. That was 300 dollars. Those who had worked were to get an extra 10 dollars. That was 80 dollars. Sparks would get 30 dollars. The three officers and the assistant Engineer would get 50 dollars each. That made 610 dollars.

"'Then,' said I, 'there's Manuel Garcia. He'll need 100 dollars.'

"'What did he do?' asked the Chief.

"'Nothing, but we sold his cargo.'

"Our expenses were 710 dollars, and the whisky had cost 10,800 dollars. A total of 11,510 dollars. For that we received 30,000 dollars.

"'A profit, Chief, of 18,490 dollars. That's over 150 per cent.'

"'It's naething of the kind. It's just over sixty per cent.'

"Next day I told the crew of the bonus. Then I added:

'It will not be paid until we leave Pernambuco. Let every man keep his mouth shut. Savvy?' They all answered 'Aye, aye, sir'. That day there was an unfortunate incident. The cook's boy ran forward to the fo'c'sle yelling: 'The cook's mad.' I was on the bridge at the time and went aft to investigate. Our cook was a huge negro. I had known him as a decent quiet man. He was no longer decent or quiet. He was stark naked and brandishing a carving-knife while he did a war-dance on the after-hatch. I called to him: 'Drop that knife, Sambo.' He gave a yell and came leaping with the knife raised towards me. In Japan I had studied ju-jitsu. It is a useful science. The stronger and heavier your adversary the easier it is to make him hurt or even kill himself. The cook only dropped his knife after he had broken his right arm at the elbow joint. Then he clenched me with his left arm. I got a double grip on him and the next time he heaved he threw himself over my shoulder and overboard. As he fell to the ditch he gave a roar that reminded me of the wounded bull buffalo I shot on the bank of the Limpopo. I went forward and asked the men if they'd seen what happened aft. 'No, sir, but the boy says the cook's mad.'

"'The cook was mad and jumped overboard. It's too rough to attempt a rescue. Any of you who can cook may volunteer for the job.'

"By careful steaming we reached Pernambuco at midnight on the following Saturday. On Sunday morning the police and Customs came on board. I signed their papers and handed the Customs a copy of our cargo list. This did not mention whisky because we had none. Before going ashore I ordered the hatch to be lifted from the after-hold. In the Grand Via I called on Manuel Garcia. He was rather puzzled and handed me the papers he had received by post. 'Señor, it was very kind of you, but I cannot pay for all this whisky.'

"You're not meant to pay. Just sign this paper.'

"'Then I sign for what I do not receive.'

"'Just so, and for your signature I give you 100 dollars.'

"'Many, many thanks, Señor'—and he signed.

"'Don't talk about this.'

"'No, Señor, I am one of the Silent Ones.'

"I went back to the ship. At 1 p.m. a representative of the ship's agents came on board to tell me the dockers would begin unloading in the morning. He was a young Englishman and seeing the open hatch said: 'Looks as if they've begun.'

"'No, Garcia sent a truck and his own men for the whisky this morning. Here's his receipt.'

"'Then he's settled with the Customs?'

"'Can you see 200 cases of whisky leaving this dockyard without the Customs?'

"He laughed. 'No indeed, Captain, I can not.'

"In a week we were on the high seas homeward bound for Liverpool."

My business friend also told me of the Captain's amazing memory. A cousin of his had returned from Trinidad where he had supervised the dredging of the harbour. "He was staying with us, and one night the Captain was invited to meet him at dinner. The two had a great talk and when the Captain left the cousin said: 'That man has a wonderful memory. He knows the depths in Trindad Harbour as well as I do.'

"'Well, he's often been there.'

"'Yes, but what a memory.'"

When the business man and his wife dined with the Captain he often wore one or other of his two mess kits. He had been a Commander R.N.R., and the Commodore of a great shipping Line. At his house they often met a small, wizened, old lady. Her name was Miss McTurk. She seldom talked and when she did it was with a Belfast accent. She helped about the house, and appeared to be an old family retainer.

The Captain's library was a remarkable room. The walls were hung with pictures and photographs of the ships in which he had sailed. Some were warships. There was the head of a buffalo. All his books were about the sea—navigation, oceanography, histories of naval wars, and a complete set of the Admiralty Sailing Directions for every coast in the world. On the mantelshelf on either side of the clock was the model of a steamer, the kind of model you see in the windows of shipping companies. These were in glass frames, and in each frame was a small silver plate which gave the date when the models had been presented to the Captain as a token of appreciation by the Chairman and Directors of the Line.

One winter's evening the Captain and my friend sat smoking by the library fire. Having gazed at his beloved models the Captain spoke: "D'ye know it's more difficult to stowaway in a small ship than on a liner. Take that ocean-going tramp. We were five days out from Valparaiso and in the Magellan Straits when the bosun brought me a stowaway. The man was so weak he could hardly stand. I cursed the bosun for not finding the man before we left Valparaiso. Then I told him to take the man to the fo'c'sle and give him food and drink. I would see him in two hours' time. He was a little man, unshaven with black hair. When I saw him again he gave his name as Carlo Sanchez. 'You come aboard at Valparaiso?'

"'Yes, Señor.'

"'What is your nationality?'

"'I do not know, Señor.'

"'Where were you born?'

"'I do not know, Señor.'

"'Where were your parents born?'

"'I do not know, Señor.'

"'Well, tomorrow you begin working your passage to Liverpool. There I hand you over to the police. They will ask you the same questions. So you'd best remember the answers.'

"The man worked well and was popular with the crew. They gave him tobacco. for he was penniless. Before we reached Liverpool I had another talk with him but learnt little more. 'Where did you want to go?'

"'To London, Señor.'

"'Know anyone there?'

"'I know one man.'

"'What's his name?'

"'Alberto Gomez.'

"'What's his address?'

"'I do not know, Señor.'

"Well, by the time we reached Liverpool I had decided not to hand him to the police. I was sorry for the poor devil. He seemed to be a stateless person, and I wanted to save myself trouble. So when the dockers were unloading I said to the man, 'See these dockers? When they knock off they'll go out of the docks by that gate. If you go with them you too may get out. Here's five pounds for you.'

"'A million thanks, Señor.'

"'Don't let me see your face again.'

"I watched him get out all right. Four days later I was in my cabin. I was reading one of the Liverpool evening papers and got the shock of my life. The London police had picked up Carlo Sanchez. He had told the Bow Street magistrate that he had come to England as a stowaway in my ship. Apparently he had not said that I helped him to land. But the fat was in the fire, and next morning I was not surprised when told to be at the Company's offices at 9.30 a.m. There I saw the Chairman and the Secretary. The Chairman said, 'You've seen the papers, Captain. What about that stowaway of yours?'

"I told him the truth and he said, 'Well, it might have been worse. The man has been moved to the Liverpool prison. Next week the police will put him on board your ship before you sail for Valparaiso. Now in view of your past services that's all you'll hear of this matter from me or from anyone else.'

"I thanked him, and next week Carlo Sanchez began working his passage back to Valparaiso. There when the police came on board I handed him over. They spoke to him in Spanish, asked the same questions I had asked, and got the same answers. Then they point-blank refused to take the man. 'No, Señor, he cannot land at Valparaiso. He has no papers. He does not know to what country he belongs.'

"'But damn it all he came on board here and he speaks Spanish.'

"'So do millions in South America and there are many countries. No, Señor, he cannot land here.'

"The British Consul could not help. A policeman watched the ship day and night. When we sailed for home I did not know what to do. Was I to spend the rest of my life carrying this man from one hemisphere to the other and back again. I thought of throwing him overboard. That would be murder, and I had never done murder. I have shot the ringleader of a mutiny. Shot him dead, but that was not murder. So I looked at the chart, and one night took the ship into a bay and anchored half a mile from the shore. Then I sent for the second officer. 'Take four men and a boat. Land the stowaway. If there's a surf don't risk yourselves on the boat. Push the man overboard and let him swim for it.'

"'Aye, aye, sir.'

"Then I had a word with the stowaway. I gave him a bottle of water, one pound of biscuits, and ten dollars. I told him there was a small town ten miles to the south. Then I ordered him into the boat. He thanked me.

"The boat pulled off. After an hour I began to get anxious. If I lost an officer, four men, and a boat on the shore of South America, I would spend the rest of my life on the beach.

"Half an hour later the boat returned and all was well. There was a heavy surf, but they found the mouth of a river and had landed the man on the south bank. That night I slept well.

"Now take my last ship—that's her up there—the liner,

twenty-two thousand tons. When I commanded her I used to go around alone at odd hours to keep an eye on things. One night about midnight I was on D deck in the First Class. I saw a man who looked like a sailor coming from an alley that led from the cabins. I stopped him and said, "Who are you?'

"'Member of the crew, sir, name John Smith.'

"'All right, walk ahead of me to the chartroom.'

"He did so. Knew the way. In the chartroom I shut the door and sat down. "Who are you?'

"'Member of the crew, sir, name John Smith.'

"'You're probably a thief.'

"'No, sir, I'm not a thief. I'm a professional stowaway.'

"'What's the difference between a professional and an amateur?'

"'Well, sir, the amateur gets caught or killed. They hide in the wrong places, such as a potato locker. After the ship sails the locker may be locked and he dies of suffocation. Others go to the engine-room and hide in the tunnel. They get mauled by the machinery. When found they're dead or dying. The engineers throw them overboard.'

"'Why?'

"'To save an inquest at the end of the voyage.'

"'And the professional?'

"'He's different, sir. He takes on board a lump of chalk, a bottle of water, and some bread. Of these the most important is the chalk. Now when I steps on board...'

"'How do you get on board?'

"'With the luggage porters or with the crews. I once got on board with the ocean pilot at Gravesend. Told him I was a member of the crew reporting late. When I steps on board I go straight below. If you hesitate an officer will stop you. They pay no attention to a man who knows where he's going.'

"'How do you know where you're going?'

"'Because you've served on the same ship or on a sister ship.

I go to the First Class and choose a lavatory. I chalks on the door the words "Out of Order". Then I pops in and bolts the door. There's a long wait. Before the pilot goes off you hear the bosun and his men searching the ship for stowaways. They never bother about a lavatory marked "Out of Order". After that you wait for night. By the sounds in the ship you can tell day from night. At night you come out and go to the fo'c'sle. There you get plenty of grub and the crew will never give you away.'

"'How about the watches?'

"'Well, sir, when the watch is called you go out with them and join the watch coming off. At the end of the voyage there's more delay. I wait two days before going ashore. Then the police are used to the crew and don't bother to ask for passes. Many a one has been caught by going ashore too soon.'

"'What do you do for a living?'

"'I breed rabbits at Birmingham, sir.'

"'Who's feeding your rabbits now.'

"'My wife, sir. This is only a holiday.'

"'Where were you going when I stopped you?'

"'To the fo'c'sle, sir.'

"'Well, you'd better go there.'

"'Thank you, sir.'

"On my next voyage before the pilot went off I told the fifth officer to find out how many lavatories were marked 'Out of Order'. He reported six. I told the bosun to open the lavatories. The pilot took ashore six stowaways. That increased my reputation on board."

When my friend had told me these stories I said, "They should be published."

"Well, I told the Captain that if he wrote his memoirs any publishers would publish them. But he said he was better at yarning than writing."

"Why not write them yourself?"

"I'm a business man, not a writer.   But you're welcome to write them."

"Many thanks, I will."

"Then you'd better have the end of the story.   It's as good as any story in *Arches of the Years*."

"I'm all ears."

"My wife and I had moved to Cork.   One afternoon Miss McTurk telephoned that she had brought the Captain in an ambulance to hospital.   She would stay a few days until the doctor found the cause of his illness.   I was very busy at the time but I telephoned the priest who attended the hospital.   I asked him to tell the Captain I would be round as soon as I could.   I also warned him that the Captain was not interested in religion.   The next evening Miss McTurk telephoned to say that the Captain was better.   It was all the more a shock when she telephoned next morning to tell me the Captain was dead.   She asked me to phone his wife and break the news. This I did.   She was very upset.   Finally she said the Captain should be buried at sea.   I agreed, and arranged for a tug to be at the docks at 9 a.m. next day.   That cost twenty pounds. Next morning Miss McTurk and I were at the docks to meet the coffin.   It came by hearse from the hospital.   The crew lashed it to the stern of the tug.   When the ropes were loosed it would fall into the sea.   Then they covered it with the Red Ensign.   Miss McTurk and I sat aft with our backs to the coffin.   The tug proceeded through the docks and down the river to Cobh.

"As we steamed through the docks Miss McTurk said, 'I suppose you don't know that you're taking part in the greatest farce of the century?'

"'What do you mean?'

"'Why are all these ships flying their flags at half-mast?'

"'That's the last tribute to a great sailor.'

"'Their last tribute to my great-grandmother!   Do you know the Captain made only one voyage in his life.   That was from England to Cork. He was so seasick that he was afraid to return.'

"I began to feel sick myself as she continued:

"'His father was a rich London stockbroker. When he died the son sold the business and became—the Captain. But that's not the worst. You're a Catholic and I am a Protestant. His wife has arranged for a Protestant clergyman to read the Burial Service. The night before he died the Captain was received into your Church.'

"'Thank God for that.'

"'Well, don't tell his wife.'

"At Cobh the wife and a clergyman joined the tug. At once the clergyman took me aside. 'I don't know whether I should be here. There's a rumour that the Captain was received into your Church before he died.'

"'Say nothing about it. You can say a few prayers. It will be all right.'

"The tug steamed out to sea. One of the crew handed out lunch. The tug stopped five miles out. The parson said a few prayers. So did I. The crew loosed the ropes and from under the Red Ensign the coffin fell with a splash into the sea. The Red Ensign was hauled on board. The tug turned back towards Cobh and Cork."

The Captain had been a paranoic. That is the modern word for systematised delusional insanity. In two ways the Captain was fortunate. His disease never went beyond the first stage of delusions. The second stage is suspicion; the third is flight; and the fourth is revenge. As a rich man he was able to buy the things that made his delusions more real to himself and to other people. Paranoics are the only happy lunatics. Very few are certified as insane. There is usually one in every London club. I wonder what would have happened to the Captain if he had really followed the sea.

CHAPTER XIII

The Catholic Church in Ireland

"WELL, Cardinal, did you meet the Irish bishops?"

"Your Holiness, there are no bishops in Ireland. There are twenty-eight popes."

This apocryphal conversation is supposed to have taken place at the Vatican in 1922 under the following circumstances. In that year the Irish bishops, having met at Maynooth, issued a statement in which they condemned the Free State Government. They said the Government should govern or resign. Some members of the Government resented the bishops' excursions into politics and complained to the Pope. So the Pope sent a Cardinal to inquire into the cause of the trouble. It may be the Cardinal was not armed with sufficient documents, but he only succeeded in seeing one member of the hierarchy, the late Archbishop of Tuam. Hence the apocryphal story.

Is that story *ben trovato?* On 3rd May, 1955, the Most Reverend Dr. Lucy, Bishop of Cork, preached a sermon on the sanctity of marriage. This sermon is reported in the *Cork Examiner* of 4th May, 1955. Concerning the limitation of families the Bishop, *inter alia,* is reported to have said: "When for any reason whatever a married couple desire not to have children the only way for them is the way of marital continence, of self-restraint."

Most people would take that to mean complete continence. If the sermon was fully and accurately reported the Bishop ignored the pronouncement by Pope Pius XI concerning the use of the 'safe' or agenetic period. He therefore gave an incomplete account of the teaching of the Catholic Church. The sermon was delivered after the Sacrament of Confirmation to presumably a congregation that included many young persons. It may be said that this was neither the time nor the occasion to refer to the 'safe' period. In that case was it either the time or the occasion to refer to the limitation of families?

Pope Pius XI in his Encyclical *Casti Connubii* dated 31st December, 1930, after a general condemnation of contraception, excludes from that condemnation the use of the 'safe' period—"nor are those to be considered as acting against nature who, in the married state use their right in the proper manner, although for natural reasons either of time or certain defects, new life cannot be brought forth. For in matrimony as well as in the use of matrimonial rights there are also secondary ends, such as mutual aid, the cultivation of mutual love, and the quieting of concupiscence, which husband and wife are not forbidden to consider so long as they are subordinated to the primary end, and so long as the intrinsic nature of the act is preserved."

Rome has now decided that before making use of the 'safe' period Catholics should consult their confessor to ensure that they have right reasons for making use of this form of birth control.

There are several differences between a Catholic parish in Britain and in Ireland. In Britain there is one church whereas in Ireland there may be many churches in one parish. In Britain the parish priest and his curate or curates live together in one house. In Ireland the curates often live in separate houses because each has his own church. There is also in Ireland a priest whose rank is lower than that of a curate. He is called a "Reader" and receives a stipend from the Church but does not share in the Christmas and Easter Offerings. In Ireland a curate may be 60 years of age before he becomes a parish priest. His curates may be men of 40 or 50. At these ages men have become set in their habits and idiosyncrasies, and that is one good reason why they should not live together.

Throughout the Catholic Church there is no compulsory retiring age for priests, bishops, cardinals, or popes. *Ad vitam aut culpam* is the rule. Recently an English Bishop called on an elderly parish priest and suggested he should retire, having reached the great age of 83.

"And how old is your Lordship?"

"All right," said the Bishop who was senior.

Last year I met an Australian priest who for the first time had visited Ireland and England. He had spent three months in each country. I asked him what he thought of the Catholic Church in these countries. He replied very frankly: "In Ireland the parish priest has too much political power. In England the hierarchy do nothing unless kicked by the laity." Be it noted that in its original meaning the word hierarchy included the laity.

In the old days the parish priest was one of the few educated men in an Irish village. He was the natural leader of his people against the Foreign Power. From Eire the Foreign Power of England has now been withdrawn and education is spreading, but the parish priest still wishes to retain his political ascendency over the people. Here be it noted that the famous song "Father O'Flynn" was written by a Protestant.

The Irish secular clergy hold themselves aloof from the people. One Irish Catholic said to me: "In Eire you will see many villages with only a single two-storied stone house. That is the priest's house, and none goes there." Another who had lived in England said: "If I were in trouble I would not hesitate to consult an English priest. I know he would do his best to help me. Here the priest would not be bothered." Another thought the priests were too prosperous. When I pointed out that I had never been asked for a collection in any Irish church, he replied: "If you lived here you'd find they were round every week." Yet another suggested that every

Irish priest should first work for four years in England. I think that most of the Irish were glad to see their priests well housed and prosperous.

At the Cork Opera House I saw *Is The Priest At Home?* This brilliant comedy, without a love interest, is by the Belfast author, Mr. Joseph Tomelty. His play suggests that the Irish people have made their priests what they are. Father Molan has been appointed the curate in charge of a church in Northern Ireland. He is a good priest and has worked four years in England. He has returned to Ireland with the firm intention of preaching The Mystical Body of Christ. The play opens on his first morning in the presbytery when Mrs. Ballafer calls to see him. She is the wife of a rich tradesman and has been accustomed to managing the parish. She invites the priest to dinner but he declines. For three months the congregation, a most uncharitable lot, wear down his intention. Finally he thinks less of the Universal Church and more of the *Ecclesia Hibernia*. The play was well acted by the Ulster Theatre Group and was enthusiastically received by a full house.

There are two practices of the Catholic Church in Ireland to which every layman objects. One is called the "Funeral Collection". I was first told of this by a retired sergeant. In the graveyard the coffin rests on trestles. Beside the coffin is a table covered with a white cloth. On this table the mourners deposit their contributions to the funeral collection. This collection is over and above the fee the priest has received from the relatives for the burial service. The priest delays the burial until he is satisfied enough money has been contributed.

"And how much does he want?"

"Well, that depends on the corpse. If it was my funeral he would expect less than for a respectable person like yourself."

Here be it noted that in Ireland the adjective "respectable" often means worldly substance, whereas in England it has a moral connotation.

I also heard of four Englishmen who bought an estate in

Ireland. One of them became converted to the Catholic Faith. When he died his brothers did not want a funeral collection to be taken at the Requiem Mass. So they saw the priest and gave him a cheque for £350. With the worst will in the world I doubt the amount of the cheque. At the Requiem they were horrified to see the white-covered table with a clerk from the local bank to count the collection. When they accused the priest of breach of faith he replied: "It's difficult to stop an old custom."

The funeral collection is certainly an old custom. It began in the Penal days when Irish Catholics were not allowed to practise their religion. When a Catholic died the English Government tolerated the presence of a priest in mufti who came to bury him. The funeral collection was then one of the ways in which the people could support their priests. The Penal days are gone but I am told funeral collections are still taken in the three north-eastern dioceses of Ireland.

When I mentioned the funeral collection to my old friend Dr. Daniel Kennedy, he said: "This is the first I have heard of such a thing; but I have known a priest to return fifteen shillings out of the one pound he had received from a poor widow for burying her husband."

Dr. Kennedy was once Medical Superintendent of the Blagdon Sanatorium, Somerset, and is godfather to my son Peter. He now lives at Kinsale where his home overlooks a beautiful but deserted harbour. We had last met in England more than thirty years ago when he motored me to a shoot in Wiltshire. He had said he was nervous all day because I had told him I had neither a gun nor a game licence and because the Chief Constable of Wiltshire was one of the shooting party. I told him he should feel confident that the Chief Constable would never ask his fellow guests to show their licences.

In County Sligo they told me that the people, if for any reason a priest could not come to the funeral, buried the dead themselves. They then took a bagful of earth to the priest and asked him to bless it. The earth they later sprinkled on the grave. As the ground was already consecrated I think they had the superstitious idea of a priest. By his ordination a priest may administer the Sacraments of the Church. In the Confessional he has the power to forgive sins; but the efficacy of the words *Ego te absolvo* depend on the dispositions of the penitent. If the confession be deliberately partial or false, the words are worthless. Indeed the penitent has added to his sins. That is the Catholic Faith.

The second practice to which the laymen object is the charge made for Letters of Freedom. When Catholics marry outside their own parish they must get from the parish priest a Letter of Freedom, which states that they are free to marry. That is Canon Law. In Britain it is customary, after getting the Letter, to make an offering to the priest. In Ireland the priest makes a charge for the Letter. An Irish lady who was to be married outside her parish went to the priest and asked for the Letter of Freedom. The following was their conversation.

"And what does your intended husband do?"

"He's a soldier, Father."

"Then it will cost you £7 10s."

To me she said: "I wonder what he would have charged had he known that my intended husband was an officer in the Irish Army."

The only excuse for this charge is that the parish priest will not officiate at the wedding. Nevertheless such a charge must make solicitors envious.

One evening when I was staying at Cobh the Chairman of the Urban District Council, Mr. Daniel Casey, accompanied by a press photographer, called to see me at the hotel. The hotel proprietor, Mr. Buckley, was also present. For ten minutes the three men discussed the ancient history of Cobh until I said: "Gentlemen, this is very interesting but I am not writing a history of Ireland."

CHAIRMAN U.D.C.: No, you want to get a general impression.

MYSELF: Precisely.

CHAIRMAN U.D.C.: You have travelled the world and . . .

MYSELF: No, no. I have not travelled the world. I have never been to the Americas, to South Africa, Russia, and the Far East.

CHAIRMAN U.D.C.: Well, you've travelled widely. Would you say we were a civilised people?

MYSELF: Yes, you are civilised, but I think that you are a priest-ridden people.

CHAIRMAN U.D.C.: And you're a Catholic?

MYSELF: Yes, I'm a Catholic, a papist, and you are Chairman of the Urban District Council.

CHAIRMAN U.D.C.: I have the honour to hold that position. Last week I opened the new Sanatorium.

MYSELF: Last year your Council unanimously agreed to build a swimming-pool at Cobh. It was to be open six days a week, alternate days for men and women. Why has it not been built?

CHAIRMAN U.D.C.: He objected.

MYSELF: You mean the Bishop of Cloyne?

CHAIRMAN U.D.C.: Yes, he's responsible for our spiritual and moral welfare.

MYSELF: How on earth could a swimming-pool, open alternately to men and women, affect your spiritual or moral welfare?

CHAIRMAN U.D.C.: He wouldn't like to see sun-bathing.

MYSELF: For that matter neither would I. After adolescence the human body, male or female, is seldom beautiful. You could have forbidden sun-bathing.

THE PHOTOGRAPHER: He's got you there.

The photographer then took a picture of the three of us. Next morning he kindly left a copy for me at the hotel.

Many of the Irish appear to have an imperfect knowledge of their religion. Among the working class some do not know the difference between the Virgin Birth and the Immaculate Conception, two dogmas of the Faith. After the First World War the Reverend Mother of a convent in East London told me the following story. They had a Day School but also had half a dozen girls as boarders. One day a Sister was talking to these girls. She pointed out that in an air raid the Jews, who abounded in that locality, always rushed to the tube station for shelter. Lest this should sound uncharitable she added: "But we should always remember Our Lord was a Jew." Then up there spoke an Irish girl aged 12: "You bold Sister! He was an Irishman and He was born in Ireland."

To this imperfect knowledge I attribute most of the leakage from the Catholic Church of those Irish who come to England. In Ireland attendance at Mass is a social duty which few miss. Indeed in the old days if a man lay abed on Sunday he might be visited by two priests who would beat him with their sticks. Today I know of one Irish village where courting couples about to take a walk in the dusk will ask: "Did you see the priest?" "Yes, he went the other way." "All right, we'll go this way." Such priests should read Maupassant's wonderful story of "Moonlight in Auvergne". In Britain attendance at Mass is a spiritual duty. Those who went to Mass in Ireland like sheep will now follow the example of 90 per cent of the British public who now do not go to any church.

In England and Wales there are estimated to be 800,000 persons who were born in Ireland. In Dublin an official of the Legion of Mary told me he estimated that of Irish migrants to Britain 25 per cent were "worthy Catholics". By this he meant that they heard Mass on Sundays and went to Holy communion once a month. Twenty-five per cent were "unworthy Catholics", that is, they only went to Mass and Holy Communion at Easter. Fifty per cent gave up their religion when they came to England. Most English priests agree with that estimate.

The Irish, Welsh and English bishops are concerned with

the fate of those Irish "exiles", who would be more correctly described as migrants. The Irish and some of the English bishops preface their remarks with a tribute to what English Catholics owe to the Irish. My wife, in her teens, was told by an Irish Christian Brother that "In Heaven the English will look over the shoulders of the Irish". Indeed, one might think that the Irish had brought Christianity to England. It is not so. England and Wales were converted by the Roman Legions. After the conversion of Constantine the Catholic Church became the Established Church of the Empire. It was St. Ninian who converted Scotland. He was the son of a Pictish Chief and had been taken to Rome as a hostage. He returned to Scotland with twelve stonemasons in 397, and at Whithorn in Galloway built the first church in Scotland. His disciple Caradoc instructed St. Patrick in the Faith before the latter went to Ireland. This is history, and I would rather hear English bishops praising the people of Lancashire who remained steadfast in the Faith throughout the Reformation.

To end this chapter I shall record the conversation between an English priest and one of the "exiles". To avoid identification the names of the churches have been changed:

"As I motored back to the parish, late one evening, a man thumbed a lift. In the dark he could not see my clerical collar, and in a rich Irish accent he said, 'Are you goin' towards the town, mate?' 'Sure,' I replied, and he got in.

"'Where are you from?' I said.

"'I live in the town.'

"'Yes, but you weren't born there.'

"'No,' says he, 'I was born in Ireland near the Border.'

"'Would you be one of those Roman Catholics?' I asked.

"'Ach! Sure!' says he. 'I'm a Roman Catholic, but I don't bother much about it. You know over there they're terrible fanatical about it all. On a Sunday morning, if I didn't get up for Mass, my Father would throw a bucket of water over me.'

"'More power to his elbow,' I said.

"'Would you be a religious man yourself, mate?' he inquired.

"'As a matter of fact,' I replied, 'I'm a Catholic priest.'

"'Mother of God!' said he.

"'And tell me,' I said, 'how long is it since you were at Mass.'

"'Oh! Father,' says he, "tis terrible rare that I miss; and then only when I have to work on Sundays.'

"'And how many Sundays do you have to work on?' I asked.

"'Eh! About one in sixteen, Father. But you know I'm living with Protestants, and there's breakfast at ten o'clock on Sunday morning.'

"'Excellent,' I replied, 'you can go to Mass and Holy Communion at eight o'clock at St. Andrew's, and be back in time for breakfast, or you can have your breakfast and go to the twelve o'clock at St. George's, and you have a bus to both churches.'

"'Well now that's interesting. But you know, Father, there's terrible persecution in England.'

"'Rubbish,' I said, 'we don't get justice for our schools, but even that bill could be paid for, if all the Irish in England went to church and gave according to their means.'

"'That's a terrible thing to say, Father, considerin' that the only churches in England that are full, are full because of the Irish that is goin' to them.'

"'Rubbish,' I shouted.

"'But it's true, Father, you can always tell the Irish at Mass.'

"'Sure,' I said, 'they come in late, stand at the back, smell of beer, and put a penny in the plate.'

"'That's not true, Father,' he said; 'at home everyone gives accordin' to his means; and it's the same over here.'

"'Rubbish,' I said, 'and tell me, have you made your Easter duties?'

There was a pause.

"'Well,' said I, 'Why haven't you made them?'

"'Tell you the truth, Father,' he said, 'I didn't know what time confessions were.'

"'Strange,' I said, 'it's written up clearly on the notice-board of the church you go to every Sunday—except one in sixteen. Besides, you can always go round to the presbytery and ask for confession.'

"'Well, I didn't know that! At home in Ireland, you can't do that and what's more if you left it more than a month, the priest would make an exhibition of you in the church.'

"'But I keep telling you that the Church is better in England than in Ireland. Such a thing would never happen here.'

"'Ah! 'twould, Father, with an Irish priest. You see, you English priests are too easy with the people.'

"'Well,' I said, 'if it means that they still go to church, if we do treat them easily, surely that's better than treating them rough, so that they don't go to church, when they leave Ireland.'

"'Ah well, Father, it's not as easy as that.'

"'Nothing ever is,' I replied, 'but confession for you is, and next Saturday, you can go to St. Andrew's, and get confession in the morning from eleven o'clock to twelve o'clock, and in the evening from six o'clock to eight o'clock; and if there is no priest about in the church, you can go round to the presbytery and ask for Father O'Brien.'

"'Ah! Sure! He'd never hear my confession out of time.'

"'He would,' I replied, 'because he's a very fine Englishman. That was a dirty one, wasn't it? Well, good night and God bless you.'

"'Good night, Father,' he said, getting out of the car, 'and t'anks for the lift.'"

CHAPTER XIV

The Irish People

"THE Irish are an honest people. They never praise each other." Dr. Johnson's dictum in the eighteenth century is true to this day. Recently I heard a symposium by half a dozen Irish friends of the late George Moore. It was on the Third Programme of the B.B.C. Each of the friends enjoyed what my daughter calls "a good pick" and at the finish the dead man was left without a feather. Although I had never read a word of what he wrote, nevertheless I felt embarrassed. Perhaps I was haunted by the old pagan maxim, *De mortuis nil nisi bonum.*

In Irish humour there is malice. This is manifest in James Joyce's *Ulysses.* I first heard of this book when a London doctor brought a copy back from Paris under his waistcoat. A week later he said the book was not pornographic. This book, banned by all the London lending-libraries, was not banned by the Irish Board of Censors. Joyce, educated by the Jesuits, is unfair to Irish Catholics when he describes a funeral in the Dublin cemetery. The mourners were preoccupied with the corruption that awaited the body they had buried. In the case of one mourner these thoughts reach a climax when he sees a rat in a vault. As a child I played in the Glasgow Necropolis when the gates were closed. I respected the graves and was not afraid of the tombstones during daylight, but never a rat did I see in that city of the dead. In any case the rat does not matter. The body rotting in the grave is mine but it is not Me. Christians believe in a life beyond the grave. They believe in the promise of Christ: "In my

Father's house there are many mansions. If not I would have told you because I go to prepare a place for you." That is the greatest lie or the greatest truth ever told to the world. Those who think that for them Death ends everything should also be unconcerned with what happens to their dead bodies. The body begins to die as soon as it has reached maturity and some of us have been dying for a long time. Between the ages of 20 and 30 I feared Death, but as we grow older we accept as inevitable what the Spaniards call, "The Last Evil, for which there is no cure." I think Renan was wrong when he wrote: "Man does not fear Death. He fears annihilation." He has more reason to fear the Judgment.

Then Joyce tells a story of two "elderly virgins", an English writer might have said "elderly spinsters", but that would have spoilt the Irish joke. They decide to visit Nelson's Pillar in O'Connell Street. For refreshment each brings a bag of prunes. On the parapet of the Pillar they eat the prunes and expectorate the stones into the street. Then they look up and see above them "the one-armed adulterer". This shows the malice of Irish humour because it mocks the physical and moral defects of a great and good man.

When I see a picture of Lady Hamilton I think of Nelson, but when I see a statue of Nelson I think of the great Admiral whose three greatest victories are now commemorated by three white stripes on the collar of every sailor of every navy of the world. In the Dublin newspapers there is an intermittent correspondence urging that the statue of Lord Nelson should be replaced by one of Our Lady! That is not Irish humour.

The English are a very tolerant people. I have never lost an appointment in England by reason of my nationality or my religion. Yet it is England's fault if she is dissatisfied with the Irish. By her fault I do not mean the Anglo-Saxon brutality that has often marred her foreign policy, but her habit of attributing to other races those qualities that England does not want for herself. "Taffy was a Welshman, Taffy was a thief."

We sang that when I was a child. Yet I have known at least
one honest Welshman. The Scots are supposed to be mean,
whereas of all races in these islands they are the most generous.
The Irish are supposed to be a carefree, rollicking, jig-dancing
people. Nothing could be further from the truth. Even
under the superficial gaiety of Dublin you can sense the innate
Celtic sadness. G. K. Chesterton in a broadcast once said that
I was one of the writers who could understand the Irish because I was Celtic. That was a very kind thing to say; but I
doubt if it was true because all my forebears came from
Caithness, which was once conquered by the Vikings as the
place names show. Thurso means the town of Thor, and
Lybster means the lobster pot. The name Sutherland means
the land south of the Ord of Caithness. Physically I am more
Norse than Celtic. At all events I think the Irish are a hard-
headed people whose business acumen is camouflaged by the
"blarney".

Bernard Shaw was an Irishman who believed that England
had attributed her own qualities to the Irish. He wrote long
introductions to his plays in order to explain what they were
about. In his introduction to *John Bull's Other Island* he
wrote: "Let me find you a more dramatic instance. Think of
the famous meeting between the Duke of Wellington, that
intensely Irish Irishman and Nelson, that intensely English
Englishman. Wellington's contemptuous disgust at Nelson's
theatricality which in an Irishman would have been an in-
sufferably vulgar affectation, was quite natural and inevitable.
Wellington's formula for that kind of thing was a well-known
Irish one: 'Sir, don't be a damned fool.' Nelson's genius
instead of producing intellectual keenness and scrupulousness,
produced mere delirium. He was drunk with glory, exalted
by his fervent faith in the sound British patriotism of the
Almighty, nerved by the vulgarest anti-foreign prejudice, and
apparently unchastened by any reflections on the fact that he
had never had to fight a technically capable and properly

equipped enemy except on land, where he had never been successful."[1]

The English language as spoken in Ireland differs from that language as spoken in England. If you ask an Irishman to come for a walk he may put on his hat and say "I might". He means "I will". In the Confessional an Irish penitent may say, "I might have taken money that was not mine." An English priest unused to the Irish idiom, will then ask, "Did you steal it?" The Irishman will reply, "Father, I might have." This means "I did", but the Irishman always prefers the oblique form of speech. Apart from this the Irish are less truthful than, let us say, the Scots. As a boy in Protestant Scotland I was taught that to tell a lie was a grievous sin; but I have heard an Irish nun describe a lie as merely a "tarradiddle". At one time I thought this untruthfulness was related to Catholicism, but now I know it is a defect of the Celtic race. The Welsh are great liars, and the people on the Western Isles of Scotland are untruthful. The Catholic Church maintains that speech was given to man in order that he might express his thoughts. So when a man says what he does not think he is violating the primary purpose of speech. Therefore a lie is a deliberate sin.

In general the Irish are a courteous people, and many of their untruths are spoken for the purpose of pleasing the visitor; although an Irishman on the make can be as brusque as a Wall Street millionaire. Also an Irishman may believe at the time what he says, but not when he has thought over it.

One night I heard an extraordinary conversation between a middle-aged doctor and an old gentleman in a pub. It was long past closing-time. Said the doctor, "I think we are a race of cowards." The old gentleman seemed slightly offended and said, "I don't know. What about the Four Courts?"

[1] *John Bull's Other Island.* Constable & Co. Ltd., Standard edition, 1947, p. 19. By permission of The Public Trustee and The Society of Authors.

DOCTOR: What about them? How many died there on Friday, June 30th, 1922?

OLD GENTLEMAN: I don't know.

DOCTOR: Neither do I, but I know that if a company of British infantry had been there, they'd be there to this day.

I took no part in that conversation. The Irish have a reputation for physical bravery. They have served as mercenaries in every army of Europe.

The Irish are puritans. They may have inherited puritanism from Cromwell. A priest told me that the greatest example of purity he had ever met was a middle-aged Irish woman who had left the Catholic Church for two years when she discovered that priests and nuns used the lavatory. I said, "Father, we are speaking different languages. What you call purity I call incredible superstition." The secular clergy have been suspected of Jansenism. This French heresy was introduced into Ireland in 1795 when the Royal College of Maynooth, founded by the English Parliament, was opened with several French priests as lecturers. Jansen published his heresy in 1622, and despite its condemnation by many Popes it persisted in France until the beginning of the present century. Pascal is its most popular exponent. Jansenists deny the freedom of the will and the possibility of resisting divine grace. In this they claimed to be restoring the ancient doctrine and discipline of the Church. They were against frequent communion except for the Elect, a word which suggests Calvinism. At the beginning of this century the Pope, Saint Pius X, advocated frequent communion for everybody including children at the age of reason. Today any eccentric overstrictness on the part of a priest is regarded as Jansenism.

The people of Eire are now divided about the partition of Ulster. Ireland should be under one Government. As the Protestant minority live at peace in the south there is no reason why the Catholic minority should not be at peace in Ulster. But there is now much unemployment in Ulster, and some Irishmen think it better that for the present the British tax-payer should bear this burden. A vociferous minority who belong to the illegal Irish Republican Army would take Ulster by force. Some of their young men have raided British garrisons in Ulster and have stolen arms in England. For these crimes they have been sentenced to long terms of penal servitude.

In Dublin I heard that the Legion of Mary had conducted a mission in Belfast. "In Belfast!" I exclaimed. I remembered my visit to that city in the nineteen-twenties and what I had heard of its Protestants. An American was there on the 12th of July. He saw a procession of Orangemen marching down the street and beating drums. They were celebrating the Battle of the Boyne. To an onlooker he said, "What's this about?"

"It's the twelfth."

"The twelfth of what?"

"The twelfth of July."

"But what happened on the twelfth of July?"

"Ach! Go home and read your bloody Bible."

Later he went to a football match between a Protestant and a Catholic team. When the Protestants played well, he cheered. Those around him smiled. When the Catholics played well he also cheered. Those around him scowled, and a man asked:

"Are you for the Catholics?"

"Not particularly."

"Are you for the Protestants?"

"Not particularly."

"Then what are you? A bloody Atheist?"

The Protestant team won the match, and on leaving the ground he overheard two Orangemen:

"A great victory."

"Yes, a great victory and tonight there will be great wailing and gnashing of teeth in the Vatican."

At the Belfast Town Hall I spoke on birth control, and prefaced my remarks by saying that Belfast would be a happier city if Catholics and Protestants remembered that they worshipped the same God and the same Saviour. The local paper printed this verbatim. Then a wild Protestant wrote to the paper to say that what I had said could not have been approved by the Catholic Church and that Protestants could not be friends with those who worshipped idols. Being young and enthusiastic I replied that we did not worship idols, and I explained the function of statues in our churches. The Protestant then wrote that Catholics had altered the Ten Commandments. He had counted the number of words dealing with the Commandments in the Catholic and Protestant Bibles. I then realised that this unhappy man believed that the Ten Commandments had been given to Moses in the English language.

"In Belfast!" I exclaimed.

"Yes," said Mr. Frank Duff, "and it was one of our most successful missions. We took a hall and advertised a lecture 'For Protestants Only'. There was a large audience, and a third of them were so interested that they wrote for further information. Then some of the Protestants held a meeting in the Town Hall on 'The Menace of Rome'. According to the Belfast paper only twenty-five attended this meeting."

Yes, it may be that the Legion of Mary will end the Ulster dispute. Politicians have been responsible for this religious bigotry.

During my last week in Dublin I visited the *Dail* where I had lunch with the Minister for Defence, General MacEion. Others told me how he had lain under sentence of death in Dublin. It was the miliatry murder of Francis Sheffington that saved him. Skeffington was known to Dublin and to Ireland as a pacifist. Yet the British military authorities put him against a wall and shot him as a *Sinn Feiner* on 26th April, 1916. His brother-in-law was then fighting for England in the trenches in France. On getting the news he wrote to Mr. John Redmond, who at once went to the Prime Minister Mr. Asquith. He telegraphed to the Commander-in-Chief General Sir John Maxwell for a full report on the execution. The reply came. It regretted that a mistake had been made. That night Mr. Asquith crossed to Dublin. Next day he saw the Commander-in-Chief and asked to see the list of those under sentence of death. This list contained the names of Eamon de Valera and of General MacEion. They were to be shot the next day. Mr. Asquith ordered that no further executions should take place. He was a good Prime Minister and he died a poor man. He was ousted from power in 1916 by the "Welsh Wizard" David Lloyd George who became Prime Minister on 6th December, 1916. The latter was responsible amongst other things for the "Black and Tans". They included the sweepings of the British Army. When the Irish gunmen shot General Wilson dead in the streets of London on 22nd June, 1922, I said they had shot the wrong man.

After lunch I had half an hour with Mr. de Valera in his private room. He is now Leader of the Opposition. It was nearly thirty years since we had met. His hair was white but he was still lean, tall and erect. He was in his 73rd year, and his eyesight had failed. As we sat he could only see my hands. He has had six operations for detachment of the retina, but is still able to write. I asked him to tell me the story of his escape from Lincoln Jail on 3rd February, 1919. With other Irish political offenders Eamon de Valera was imprisoned in Lincoln Jail. In the prison he was sacristan to the Catholic Chapel. He thought that the priest as a prison official must have a master key. This became apparent when the priest left his keys in the sacristy while officiating in the chapel. How was an impression to be made? With stumps from the altar candles. These de Valera placed in a tobacco box which he put in his pocket until the wax softened and formed a homogeneous surface. The prisoners, unlike ordinary convicts, were not searched. Thus he got an impression of the master key. How was a duplicate key to be made? One of the Irishmen was an artist, and he drew a double Christmas card. One side showed a tipsy man trying to get a large key into the door of his house. This bore the title "He wants to get in". The other side showed a convict trying to get a large key into the lock of his cell. It bore the title "He wants to get out". Both keys were drawn to scale. This card was sent to a sympathiser outside. In due course a Christmas cake arrived for de Valera. Inside the cake was a duplicate key.

The shaft of this key broke in the lock the first time de Valera tried to use it. Fortunately the business end had not turned in the lock and he was able to push it out on the other side. By this time the Irish prisoners were joined by a man who said that if they could unscrew the front of the lock he could make a key that would fit. With his typewriter de Valera had a small screw-driver. The man made two keys because it had been agreed that the others should escape as soon as de Valera was out of the country.

On a dark night de Valera left the prison by a side gate that opened on to a field. At the other side of the field was a sentry-box from which a sentry was supposed to guard that side of the prison. The gate had corrugated iron attached to the foot, and this made a great noise when being dragged over the stones. He closed and locked the gate behind him. All round the gate was barbed wire. Within the wire he saw Michael Collins and Harry Boland. They were rebuked by de Valera. It would be triumph enough for the British Government if he were recaptured. It would be a greater triumph if they captured three Irish leaders. He had only asked that a responsible man should be there as a guide. Then they had cut the barbed wire. That would show the prison authorities how he had escaped.

All three went undetected from Lincoln to Manchester. From Manchester de Valera went to Liverpool, where a steward put him on board a liner as a stowaway. In a week he was free in New York.

"Publishers must have offered you a lot for your autobiography?"

"They have, but I won't write it. You see, many of the people are dead, and I would not care to write against them."

"Then you will leave it to history."

"Well, when Miss O'Connell (his secretary) gets better I might dictate something."

Miss Kathleen O'Connell did not get better. She died, aged 67, on 17th April, 1956.

When I left the Dail I remembered that I had forgotten to ask Mr. de Valera if he had received my letter of July, 1940, because I had been told he did not answer letters. My letter was taken to Ireland by Mr. Dulanty, the Irish High Commissioner in London. In the letter I suggested to Mr. de Valera that he, without consulting the British Government, should ask the Governments of Canada and of Australia each to send an Irish Division to defend Eire. Even the anti-British Irish Republican Army could not object to Irishmen defending Ireland.

I am told that up to the middle of 1941 the Government of Eire feared that Germany, with the help of the Irish Republican Army, might get an air base in Eire. In that event it would have been a poor look-out for Liverpool and Cardiff. Members of the Irish Republican Army tell me that Eire had nothing to fear from Germany. They feared that Mr. Churchill would ask the United States Navy to seize the Irish ports.

The ports had been returned to Eire in 1938. In that year the English Prime Minister, Mr. Neville Chamberlain, believed that we would have "Peace in our time"; but Mr. Churchill and others believed that Germany was spoiling for war.

On my last day in Dublin I had lunch at the Shelbourne with General Costello, the Managing Director of the Irish Sugar Company. The Company was formed in 1933 after the passage of the Sugar Manufacture Act. Its capital is £2,000,000 sterling. All the issued Ordinary Shares of the Company are held by the Minister of Finance, save fourteen which were allotted to the first seven Directors of the Company. The public hold 500,000 6 per cent Cumulative Preference Shares of £1 each. The Company employs nearly 3,000 workmen. In 1954 farmers had put 73.507 acres under sugar-beet. The Irish Government pays £25 per acre to anyone who makes bog land cultivable. The Company drains the peat land with drains six foot deep and removes the top soil. The acidity of the peat is then treated by a dressing of lime. In this way the peat soil may bear alternate crops of sugar-beet and of grass. The Chairman of the Company, Mr. John E. McEllin in his annual report for 1953 made the following reference to Irish Agriculture:

"The serious consequences, social and economic, which followed the reduction in the tillage area from 2,314,304 acres in 1947 to 1,720,024 acres in 1952 are only now being fully felt. Even yet the effects do not seem to be sufficiently realised in many quarters, especially in the cities and towns. Its most immediate consequence has been to accelerate greatly the flight from the rural area. There is naturally a very big reduction in the numbers permanently employed on farms on which the area under tillage has been reduced. This great exodus of rural workers was accentuated by the increased demand for labour by building firms in cities and towns. The higher wage rates available to building workers and the much greater possibilities of young married couples securing housing accommodation in urban areas were also factors operating in the same direction.

"A less important factor was the rapid increase in the mechanisation of tillage operations in Ireland. This mechanisation is inevitable and, indeed, essential in order to lower the cost of production and increase the output per worker on the land. It is only such increased output that will make possible the payment of increased wages to offset the economic attractions of urban areas. As recently as 1950, the position was that the net output per head of the active agricultural population in Ireland was lower than that of any country in Europe other than Italy, Greece and Finland.

"As production per worker increases in value, the possibility of providing profitable employment for more workers in agriculture increases. By an increased tillage area, and a great intensification of dairying, of pig and poultry production, of fruit and vegetable raising, and of crops to provide industrial raw materials, the present trend could be reversed, and a great increase could take place in the number of productive workers on the land. Not merely could those replaced by the machine find profitable and productive work, but many new workers could be provided for as well.

"It would also be necessary so to diversify farming on a carefully planned pattern as to provide for a steady labour demand throughout the year, and thus avoid the peak demands now leading to acute difficulties."

After the Second World War Mr. Churchill broadcast on the B.B.C. the following speech on 13th May, 1945 :[1]

"Owing to the action of Mr. de Valera, so much at variance with the temper and instinct of thousands of southern Irishmen, who hastened to the battle-front to prove their ancient valour, the approaches which the southern Irish ports and airfields could so easily have guarded were closed by the hostile aircraft and U-boats.

"This was indeed a deadly moment in our life, and if it had not been for the loyalty and friendship of Northern Ireland, we

[1] Ireland's Stand. Selected Speeches by Eamon de Valera. Dublin, p. 80.

should have been forced to come to close quarters with Mr. de Valera, or perish for ever from the earth.

"However, with a restraint and poise to which, I venture to say, history will find few parallels, His Majesty's Government never laid a violent hand upon them, though at times it would have been quite easy and quite natural, and we left the de Valera Government to frolic with the German and later with the Japanese representatives to their hearts' content.

"When I think of these days, I think also of other episodes and personalities, I think of Lieutenant-Commander Esmonde, V.C.; Lance-Corporal Keneally, V.C.; Capt, Fegen, V.C., and other Irish heroes that I could easily recite, and all bitterness by Britain for the Irish race dies in my heart.

"I can only pray that, in years which I shall not see, the shame will be forgotten and the glories will endure, and that the peoples of the British Isles and of the British Commonwealth of Nations will walk together in mutual comprehension and forgiveness."

In the course of an address from Radio Eireann four days later (May 17th) Mr. de Valera said:[1]

"Mr. Churchill makes it clear that, in certain circumstances, he would have violated our neutrality and that he would justify his action by Britain's necessity. It seems strange to me that Mr. Churchill does not see that this, if accepted, would mean that Britain's necessity would become a moral code and that when this necessity became sufficiently great, other people's rights were not to count.

"Surely Mr. Churchill must see that if his contention be admitted in our regard, a like justification can be framed for similar acts of aggression elsewhere and no small nation adjoining a great Power could ever hope to be permitted to go its own way in peace.

"It is indeed fortunate that Britain's necessity did not reach

[1] *Ibid.*, p. 81.

the point when Mr. Churchill would have acted. All credit to him that he successfully resisted the temptation which, I have no doubt, many times assailed him in his difficulties and to which I freely admit many leaders might have easily succumbed. It is, indeed, hard for the strong to be just to the weak, but acting justly always has its rewards.

"Mr. Churchill is proud of Britain's stand alone, after France had fallen and before America entered the war.

"Could he not find in his heart the generosity to acknowledge that there is a small nation that stood alone not for one year or two, but for several hundred years against aggression: that endured spoliations, famines, massacres in endless succession; that was clubbed many times into insensibility, but that each time on returning consciousness, took up the fight anew; a small nation that could never be got to accept defeat and has never surrendered her soul?

"Mr. Churchill is justly proud of his nation's perseverance against heavy odds. But we in this island are still prouder of our people's perseverance for freedom through all the centuries. We of our time have played our part in that perseverance, and we have pledged ourselves to the dead generations who have preserved intact for us this glorious heritage, that we too will strive to be faithful to the end, and pass on this tradition unblemished.

"Many a time in the past there appeared little hope, except that hope to which Mr. Churchill referred, that by standing fast, a time would come when, to quote his own words, 'the tyrant would make some ghastly mistake which would alter the whole balance of the struggle'.

"I sincerely trust, however, that it is not thus our ultimate unity and freedom will be achieved, though as a younger man I confess I prayed even for that, and indeed, at times, saw no other.

"Meanwhile, even as a partitioned small nation, we shall go on and strive to play our part in the world, continuing unswervingly to work for the cause of true freedom, and for peace and understanding between all nations.

"As a community which has been mercifully spared from all the major sufferings as well as from the blinding hates and rancours engendered by the present war, we shall endeavour to render thanks to God by playing a Christian part in helping so far as a small nation can, to bind up some of the gaping wounds of suffering humanity.

"Agus anois, caithfidh mé slán a fhágáil agaibh. Nuair a bhíos ag caint libh i dtús an chonhaidh, chuireas an tír agus a muinntir faoi choimirce Dé agus a Mháthar Muire, agus ise mo ghuidhe anocht: Go raibh an choimrí chumhachtach chéanna oraibh san aimsir atá romhainn!"

It is, I think, clear that if Mr. de Valera had not proclaimed Eire to be neutral, the Irish Republican Army would have started a civil war and might have invited Germany to occupy that country.

To end this book I repeat what I said several years ago. There can be no peace between England and Ireland until England remembers and Ireland forgets. I would add that the Irish look backwards and the Scots look forward. Unbeknown to me Horace Plunkett in his book *Ireland in the New Century*, published in 1904, had written: "Anglo-Irish history is for Englishmen to remember, for Irishmen to forget."

To aid forgetfulness Britain should return to Eire the Lane collection of paintings, now in the Tate Gallery, and the body of Sir Roger Casement. Eire has a moral right to the former and to the latter a legal right.